# *The Book of JOB*

TRANSLATED AND WITH AN INTRODUCTION BY

*Stephen Mitchell*

NORTH POINT PRESS · SAN FRANCISCO

An earlier version of this translation was published as *Into the Whirlwind* (Doubleday, 1979). The Introduction first appeared in *Tikkun* (May, 1986).

Library of Congress Catalogue Card Number: 86-62829
ISBN: 0–86547–286–6 (cloth) / 0–86547–270–x (paper)
FIFTH PRINTING

Cover illustration: William Blake, "When the Morning Stars Sang Together," from the Illustrations to the Book of Job, © The Pierpont Morgan Library, 1987.

North Point Press
850 Talbot Avenue
Berkeley, California
94706

TO MY MOTHER AND FATHER

# Introduction

## I

One of the milder paradoxes that shape this greatest Jewish work of art is that its hero is a Gentile. Its author may have been as well. We know nothing about him, nothing about his world; he is even more anonymous than Homer. With Homer, at least, we can picture a society of competing principalities, each with its warriors and court and ceremonial feasts where the bard recites his ancient songs to the accompaniment of the lyre, like blind Demodocus in the *Odyssey*. But there is not the slightest bit of evidence about the author of *Job*: not when or where he wrote, or for what kind of audience. When we try to imagine him, we are left with a blank, or with one of those patriarchal figures dressed in bright monochrome robes who suddenly appear, devout and straight-nosed, between the pages of illustrated Bibles.

Yet however foreign the poet originally was, his theme is the great Jewish one, the theme of the victim. "Someone must have slandered J., because one morning he was arrested, even though he had done nothing wrong." That is what makes *Job* the central parable of our post-Holocaust age, and gives such urgency to its deep spiritual power.

## II

When the great Tao is forgotten,
goodness and piety appear.
TAO TE CHING

To introduce his poem, the author retells a legend that was already ancient centuries before he was born. It concerns a righteous man who for no reason has been deprived of all the rewards of his righteousness; in the midst of great suffering he remains steadfast and perfectly pious, still blessing the Lord as before. "You have heard of the patience of Job," the Epistle of James says, and it is this legendary, patient Job—not the desperate and ferociously impatient Job of the poem—who, ironically enough, became proverbial in Western culture.

We can respect the legend on its own naive terms, and can appreciate the skill with which the author retells it: the chilling conversations in heaven; the climax where Job submits, as if he were a calmer, more insightful Adam who has just eaten the bitter fruit of the Tree of Knowledge and, eyes opened, sees that he is naked. But if we read the prologue more seriously, less objectively, we may be slightly repulsed by its hero's piety. There is something so servile about him that we may find ourselves siding with his impatient wife, wanting to shout, *Come on, Job; stand up like a man; curse this god, and die!* The character called "the Lord" can do anything to him— have his daughters raped and mutilated, send his sons to Auschwitz—and he will turn the other cheek. This is not a matter of spiritual acquiescence, but of mere capitulation to an unjust, superior force.

When we look at the world of the legendary Job with a probing, disinterestedly satanic eye, we notice that it is suffused with anxiety. Job is afraid of God, as well he might be. He avoids evil because he realizes the penalties. He is a perfect moral businessman: wealth, he knows, comes as a reward for playing by the rules, and goodness is like money in the bank. But, as he suspects, this world is thoroughly unstable. At any moment the currency can change, and the Lord, by handing Job over to the power of evil, can declare him bankrupt. No wonder his mind is so uneasy. He worries about making the slightest mistake; when he has his children come for their annual purification, it is not even because they may have *committed* any sins, but may have had blasphemous *thoughts*. The superego is riding high. And in fact, at the climax of his first speech in the poem, Job confesses that his "worst fears have happened; / [his] nightmares have come to life." This is not a casual statement, added as a poetic flourish. Anxieties have a habit of projecting themselves from psychological into physical reality. Job's premonition turned out to be accurate; somewhere he knew that he was precariously balanced on his goodness, like a triangle on its apex, just waiting to be toppled over. There is even a perverse sense of relief, as if that heavy, responsible patriarch-world had been groaning toward deliverance. For any transformation to occur, Job has to be willing to let his hidden anxieties become manifest. He must enter the whirlwind of his own psychic chaos before he can hear the Voice.

As Maimonides was the first to point out, Job is a good man, not a wise one. The ascription of "perfect integrity," which both the narrator and "the Lord" make, seems valid only in a limited sense. The Hebrew says *tam v'-yashar,* which literally means "whole (blameless) and upright." Well, yes: Job has never committed even the most venial sin, in action or in thought. (For that very reason, his later agony and bewilderment are more terrible than Josef K.'s in *The Trial.*) In a broader sense, though, Job is not whole. He is as far from spiritual maturity as he is from rebellion. Rebelliousness—the passionate refusal to submit—is, in fact, one of the qualities we admire in the Job of the poem:

> Be quiet now—let *me* speak;
>     whatever happens will happen.
> I will take my flesh in my teeth,
>     hold my life in my hands.
> He [God] may kill me, but I won't stop;
>     I will speak the truth, to his face.

If we compare the legendary figure with the later Job, especially in the great summation that concludes the central dialogue, we can recognize that even his virtue lacks a certain generosity and wholeheartedness. That is why the bet doesn't prove much. Job is too terrorized, from within his squalor, to do anything *but* bless the Lord: for all he knows, there might be an even more horrible consequence in store. The real test will come later, in the poem, when he feels free to speak with all of himself, to say *any*thing.

There is a further irony about *tam v'-yashar.* When Job is handed over to the good graces of the Accuser, he is turned into the opposite of what the words mean in their most physical sense. He becomes *not-whole:* broken in body and heart. He becomes *not-upright*: pulled down into the dust by the gravity of his anguish.

The author moves us to heaven after the prologue's first scene, and we may be tempted to admire his boldness. But heaven, it turns out, is only the court of some ancient King of Kings, complete with annual meetings of the royal council and a Satan (or Accusing Angel). As below, so above. Jung, in his *Answer to Job*, makes the point that, psychologically, the Accuser is the embodiment of "the Lord's" doubt. In a more naive version of the legend, the god in his divine myopia would himself doubt the disinterestedness of his obedient human and would decide to administer the test on his own. Here, though the Accuser ostensibly plays the role of the villain, it is "the Lord" who provokes him. "Did you notice my servant Job?" How can the Accuser not take up the challenge? After all, that's his job.

As Jung also points out, this god is morally much inferior to the prologue's hero. We would have to be insensitive or prejudiced not to be nauseated by the very awareness of "the Lord's" second statement to the Accuser: "He is holding on to his wholeness, even after you made me torment him for no reason," and by the calm cruelty of "All right: he is in your power. Just don't kill him."

Nevertheless, if we want to be serious about the poem, we mustn't take the legend too seriously. There is a profound shift when the verse dialogue begins; the change in language is a change in reality. Compared to Job's laments (not to mention the Voice from the Whirlwind), the world of the prologue is two-dimensional, and its divinities are very small potatoes. It is like a puppet show. The author first brings out the patient Job, his untrusting god, and the chief spy/prosecutor, and has the figurines enact the ancient story in the puppet theater of his prose. Then, behind them, the larger curtain rises, and flesh-and-blood actors begin to voice their passions on a life-sized stage. Finally, the vast, unnamable God appears. How could the author have returned to the reality of the prologue for an answer to the hero of the poem? That would have meant "the Lord" descending from the sky to say, *Well, you see, Job, it all happened because I made this bet* . . .

No, the god of the prologue is left behind as utterly as the never-again-mentioned Accuser, swallowed in the depths of human suffering into which the poem plunges us next.

## III

If you bring forth what is inside
you, what you bring forth will
save you.

THE GOSPEL
ACCORDING TO THOMAS

When Job discovers his voice after the long silence, he doesn't curse God explicitly, as the Accuser said he would. But he comes as close as possible. He curses his own life, and in doing so curses all of life—an ultimate blasphemy for those who believe that life is an ultimate good. (We may recall another great sufferer, Oedipus at Colonus, whose chorus offers something very similar to Job's death-wish as its wisdom: It is best never to have been born; next best is to leave the womb and die immediately.) In his curse, Job allies himself with the primal forces of darkness and chaos, and with the archetypal symbol of evil, the Serpent Leviathan, whom we will meet again at the poem's conclusion. It is a ferocious hymn of de-creation. He must hurtle to the bottom of his despair before he can begin to stand up for himself.

At the end of the prologue, when they are introduced to us, the three friends who come to comfort Job are entirely correct in their behavior. How much delicacy and compassion we can feel in the author's brief account: "Then they sat with him for seven days and seven nights. And no one said a word, for they saw how great his suffering was." But they can't remain silent once Job becomes active in his anguish. Theirs is the harshest of comforting. They don't understand that Job's curses and blasphemies are really cries of pain. They *can't* understand, because they won't risk giving up their moral certainties. Their rigid orthodoxy surrounds an interior of mush, like the exoskeleton of an insect. Unconsciously they know that they have no experience of God. Hence their acute discomfort and rage.

The friends and Job all agree that God is wise and can see into the hearts of men. He is not the kind of character who would allow a good man to be tortured because of a bet; nor is he a well-intentioned bungler. Given this premise, they construct opposite syllogisms. The friends: *Suffering comes from God. God is just. Therefore Job is guilty.* Job: *Suffering comes from God. I am innocent. Therefore God is unjust.* A third possibility is not even thinkable: *Suffering comes from God. God is just. Job is innocent.* (No *therefore.*)

Even if the friends are right about God's justice, their timing is bad. In fact, they don't speak to Job at all, they speak to their own terror at the thought of Job's innocence. And though they defend God's justice, they can't afford to understand what it is. "If the wrong man says the right thing, it is wrong." So they are driven to their harsh God-the-Judge and their harsh judgments, like greater men after them who tried to justify the ways of God to men.

Any idea about God, when pursued to its extreme, becomes insanity. The idea of a just God absorbs all justice into it and leaves a depraved creation. Like proto-Calvinists, the friends extend their accusation of guilt to all mankind. Man becomes "that vermin, who laps up filth like water," and their god is revealed as a Stalin-esque tyrant so pure that he "mistrusts his angels / and heaven stinks in his nose."

Ultimately the dialogue is not about theological positions but human reactions. Afraid of any real contact with Job and his grief, the friends stay locked inside their own minds. The same arguments are recycled again and again, with more and more stridency, until they become merely boring. In the third round of the dialogue, in fact, the text itself becomes defective, as if it had broken down from the force of the friends' stuttering rage.

What makes their arguments bearable, and sometimes even thrilling, is the power of language that the poet has granted them. In this he has acted with the instinctive generosity of all great poets, endowing the friends with a life and passion almost as intense as Job's. His language is the most concrete of poetic idioms. Every idea or emotion has become an image, so vivid and

sinewy that verse after verse fills the reader with an almost physical delight. Thus Bildad, talking about the
wicked man's precarious safety:

> His peace of mind is gossamer;
> his faith is a spider's web.

Or Eliphaz, asking Job how he can be so sure he is right:

> Are you the first man to be born,
> created before the mountains?
> Have you listened in at God's keyhole
> and crept away with his plans?

Or Zophar, in disgust:

> But a stupid man will be wise
> when a cow gives birth to a zebra.

The friends, nevertheless, are supporting actors, and
our attention is focused on Job. His speeches are a kalei-
doscope of conflicting emotions, addressed to the friends,
to himself, to God. His attitude shifts constantly, and
can veer to its direct opposite in the space of a few
verses, the stream of consciousness all at once a torrent.
He wants to die; he wants to prove that he is innocent;
he wants to shake his fist at God for leaving the world in
such a wretched shambles. God is his enemy; God has
made a terrible mistake; God has forgotten him; or
doesn't care; God will surely defend him, against God.
His question, the harrowing question of someone who
has only heard of God, is "Why me?" There is no answer, because it is the wrong question. He will have to

struggle with it until he is exhausted, like a child crying itself to sleep.

In these speeches it is obvious that Job is a different character from the patient hero of the legend. He is no longer primarily a rich man bereft of his possessions and heartbroken over his dead children (they are mentioned only once in the poem). He has become Everyman, grieving for all of human misery. He suffers not only his own personal pain, but the pain of all the poor and despised. He is himself afflicted by what God has done to the least of these little ones.

In a wonderfully ironic sense, the Accuser's dirty work has resulted in an epidemic of accusations. Once that archetypal figure disappears, he is absorbed into the poem as if by some principle of the conservation of energy. The more the friends become Job's accusers, the more Job becomes the accuser of God. His outrage at the world's injustice is directed straight to the creator of that world. There are no detours or half-measures, no attempt to deflect ultimate responsibility by blaming a devil or an original sin.

> He [God] does not care; so I say
>     he murders both the pure and the wicked.
> When the plague brings sudden death,
>     he laughs at the anguish of the innocent.
> He hands the earth to the wicked
>     and blindfolds its judges' eyes.
>     Who does it, if not he?

This may be blasphemy, but it is true. Job's straightforwardness is itself a kind of innocence, and is what the god of the epilogue refers to when he tells the friends,

"You have not spoken the truth about me, as my servant Job has."

All this bewilderment and outrage couldn't be so intense if Job didn't truly love God. He senses that in spite of appearances there is somewhere an ultimate justice, but he doesn't know where. He is like a nobler Othello who has been brought conclusive evidence that his wife has betrayed him: his honesty won't allow him to disbelieve it, but his love won't allow him to believe it. On the spikes of this dilemma he must remain impaled. That is what makes his cry so profoundly moving.

The Book of Job is the great poem of moral outrage. It gives voice to every accusation against God, and its blasphemy is cathartic. How liberating it feels *not* to be a good, patient little God-fearer, scuffling from one's hole in the wall to squeak out a dutiful hymn of praise. Job's own voice has freed him so that he can move from the curses of his first speech to the final self-affirmation as his own attorney for the defense. There, with oaths of the gravest dignity and horror, he becomes upright again in his wish to "stand before [God] like a prince." It is this passionate insistence that carries him into the eye of the whirlwind. "Blessed are those who hunger and thirst after righteousness," as another Jewish teacher said, "for they shall be filled."

Of course, the answer Job receives is anything but what he expected. Heart-stirring as the summation is, he remains lost in his own concepts, and there is no small irony to his final plea, "If only God would hear me." For if we needed a sensory metaphor to describe the experience of intimacy, hearing might be the last sense we would choose. No, far more than vindication will occur: a plea will be granted that Job wouldn't have dared to make, a question answered that he wouldn't have known how to ask. God will not hear Job, but Job will see God.

## IV

To men some things are good
and some are bad. But to God, all
things are good and beautiful and
just.

HERACLITUS

If God's answer comes from an objective whirlwind, it answers nothing, and can only be the magnificent, harsh, and notoriously unsatisfactory harangue that most interpreters have found. As rational discourse, it reduces itself to this: *How dare you question the creator of the world? Shut up now, and submit.* After several pages of eloquent browbeating, Job can do nothing but squeak what amounts to, *Yes sir, Boss. Anything you say.* God apparently wants the unquestioning piety of the friends, and Job returns to the exact position he had at the end of the prologue, cringing in the dust. Compared with the endings of the *Iliad* or the *Commedia* or any of the major works of Shakespeare, this would be a wretched climax: so uneconomical, so anticlimactic indeed, that it seems more like a pratfall than a finale. We need to penetrate more deeply.

What does it mean to answer someone about human suffering? For there *are* answers beyond the one-size-fits-all propositions of the theologians. But these answers can't be imposed from the outside. They will resonate only where the questioner lets them enter. Above all, they require a willingness to accept what can be excruciating to the ego. Often we find such reality unbearable. The light is so brilliant that it hurts, as in the Tibetan Book of the Dead, and we retreat to the softer glow of a familiar, comfortable grief.

There is never an answer to the great question of life and death, unless it is my answer or yours. Because ultimately it isn't a question that is addressed, but a person. Our whole being has to be answered. At that point, both question and answer disappear, like hunger after a good meal.

"God is subtle, but not malicious," Einstein said in a different context. We have to listen to the Voice from the Whirlwind in a more oblique mode, as if its true meaning lay inside the logical framework of its words. First, we should notice how the answer consists mostly of questions (a good Jewish trait). In their volume and insistence, these questions acquire a peculiar quality. They sound in our ears as a ground bass to the melody of their content, and eventually function as a kind of benign subliminal message, asking a fundamental question that will dissolve everything Job thought he knew.

The closest we can get to that question is *What do you know?* During their dialogue, Job and the friends agree about the limits of human understanding, but none of them suspects how absolute those limits are. In order to approach God, Job has to let go of all ideas about God: he must put a cloud of unknowing (as a medieval Christian author expressed it) between himself and God, or have the Voice do this for him.

The content of the Voice's questions, aside from their rhetorical form, gives another kind of answer. Each verse presents Job with an image so intense that, as Job later acknowledges, he doesn't hear but *sees* the Voice. He is taken up into a state of vision, and enters a world of primal energy, independent of human beings, which includes what humans might experience as terrifying or evil: lightning, the primordial sea, hungry lions on the prowl, the ferocious war-horse, the vulture feeding his young with the rotting flesh of the slain. Violence, deprivation, or death form the context for many of these pictures, and the animals are to them as figure is to ground. The horse exults *because* of the battle; without the corpses, the vulture couldn't exist in his grisly solicitude. We are among the most elemental realities, at the center of which there is an indestructible power, an indestructible joy.

This worldview stands, of course, in direct opposition to the Genesis myth in which man is given dominion over all creatures. It is a God's-eye view of creation *before* man, beyond good and evil, marked by the innocence of a mind that has stepped outside the circle of human values. (When I was a very young Zen student, caught up in the problem of evil, I once asked my teacher, "Why does shit smell so bad?" He said, "If you were a fly, it would taste like candy.")

There is another text that can be contrasted: the peaceable kingdom of First Isaiah, where the wolf lies down with the lamb. Beside Job's vision, this seems a naive version of paradise, and as elusive as its direct descendent, the Marxist End-of-Days. Since Isaiah still equates the humane with the human, his desire turns the wilderness into a zoo, stocked with nonviolent wolves and vegetarian lions. The Voice, however, doesn't moralize. It has the clarity, the pitilessness, of nature and of all great art. Is the world of flesh-eaters really a demonic parody of God's intent? And what about our compassion for the prey? Projecting our civilized feelings onto the antelope torn apart by lions, we see mere horror: nature red in tooth and claw. But animals aren't victims, and don't feel sorry for themselves. The lioness springs without malice; the torn antelope suffers and lets go; each plays its role in the sacred game. When we watch from the periphery, as in a television film, we can sense the dignity this relationship confers on both hunter and hunted, even in the midst of great pain.

What the Voice means is that paradise isn't situated in the past or future, and doesn't require a world tamed or edited by the moral sense. It is our world, when we perceive it clearly, without eating from the Tree of the Knowledge of Good and Evil. It is an experience of the Sabbath vision: looking at reality, the world of starving children and nuclear menace, and recognizing that it is very good. In the fourteenth of his *Job* etchings, Blake drew small sketches of the first six days of creation in the margin (up to but not including the creation of man) and in the center, above God, he drew the angels who embody seventh-day consciousness, illustrating one of the most beautiful verses in all literature: *b'rôn-yáḥad kōkhváy vôker / vayarî'u kôl-b'náy elohîm* ["while the morning stars burst out singing / and the angels shouted for joy!"]

If we pay attention to the images themselves, we perceive an attitude, not an argument. Each metaphor describing creation in human terms has a large, ironic humor to it. As if God were really a gigantic carpenter, measuring the earth with a cord, cutting a path for the thunderstorm, etc. How else can he talk to Job about such cosmic energies, except in Job's language and with a cosmic amusement? Poignancy and humor are the essence of these images: the rain falling in the desert and for a brief time making the whole landscape spring into life and color, not for the sake of any human eye; the thunderclouds and lightning bolts hypothetically lining up like Disney cartoon figures to do Job's bidding; light and darkness as lost waifs who need to be escorted home; the wild ass that wanders in continual hunger and yet laughs at its enslaved cousins in the cities of men; the fierce exultation of the war-horse:

> Do you give the horse his strength?
>> Do you clothe his neck with terror?
> Do you make him leap like a locust,
>> snort like a blast of thunder?
> He paws and champs at the bit;
>> he exults as he charges into battle.
> He laughs at the sight of danger;
>> he does not wince from the sword
> or the arrows nipping at his ears
>> or the flash of spear and javelin.
> With his hooves he swallows the ground;
>> he quivers at the sound of the trumpet.
> When the trumpet calls, he says "Ah!"
>> From far off he smells the battle,
>> the thunder of the captains and the shouting.

We have here a whole world of the most vivid, exuberant life, where every being is the center of an infinite circle. It is far from the human-centered world of final causes that we find in the rest of the Bible. The only parallel to it in Western literature is Whitman's "Song of Myself."

Job's first response is awe. He can barely speak. He puts his hand over his mouth, appalled at his ignorance.

But there is more to come. The Voice now, in a series of gruff, most ironical questions, begins to speak explicitly about good and evil. *Do you really want this moral sense of yours projected onto the universe?* it asks, in effect. *Do you want a god who is only a larger version of a righteous judge, rewarding those who don't realize that virtue is its own reward and throwing the wicked into a physical hell? If that's the kind of justice you're looking for, you'll have to create it yourself. Because that is not* my *justice.*

The answer concludes with a detailed presentation of two creatures, the Beast and the Serpent. These have certain similarities with the hippopotamus and the crocodile, especially the herbivorous, river-dwelling Beast, which is depicted in a distinctly Egyptian landscape. But the images are hardly naturalistic, and become less so as we move from the phallic Beast to the huge, fire-breathing, invulnerable Serpent. Both creatures are, in fact, central figures in ancient near-eastern eschatology, the embodiments of evil that the sky-god battles and conquers at the end of time, just as he conquered the sea and the forces of chaos in creating the world at the beginning of time. (In the cozier mythology of the early rabbis, the good Lord, after killing the two beasts, slices and serves them up to the righteous at the never-ending banquet that is heaven.)

This final section of the Voice from the Whirlwind is

a criticism of conventional, dualistic theology. *What is all this foolish chatter about good and evil,* the Voice says, *about battles between a hero-god and some cosmic opponent? Don't you understand that there* is *no one else in here?* These huge symbols of evil, so terrifying to humans who haven't seen, or won't acknowledge, the destructive Shiva-aspect of God, are presented to us as God's playthings. They are part of the continuum of nature, which runs seamlessly from angel to beast. "The roaring of lions," as Blake wrote, "the howling of wolves, the raging of the stormy sea, and the destructive sword, are portions of *eternity* too great for the eye of man." Job's vision ought to give a healthy shock to those who believe in a moral God. The only other source in the Bible that approaches it in kilowatts is a passage from the anonymous prophet known as Second Isaiah: "I form light and create darkness; I make peace and create evil; I the Unnamable do all these things."

These passages may remind us of the radiant, large-hearted verse in which Jesus of Nazareth gives his reason for loving our enemies: "That you may be children of your father who is in heaven: for he makes his sun rise on the evil and on the good, and sends his rain on the just and on the unjust." Though in *Job* even the concept of God as a father (or mother) is gently mocked, not only in the metaphor of the primal sea being wrapped in swaddling clothes, but in the tender and very beautiful verses about the rain:

> Does the rain have a father?
>     Who has begotten the dew?
> Out of whose belly is the ice born?
>     Whose womb labors with the sleet?

*Does* the rain have a father? The whole meaning is in the *lack* of an answer. If you say yes, you're wrong. If you say no, you're wrong. God's humor here is rich and subtle beyond words.

## V

Considering that, all hatred driven hence,
The soul recovers radical innocence
And learns at last that it is self-delighting,
Self-appeasing, self-affrighting,
And that its own sweet will is Heaven's will.

YEATS

We come now to Job's final speech. To misunderstand it will be to miss his transformation and to destroy the harmonic structure that gives a book its meaning. If Job's response is unworthy, then God's answer is unworthy. One is a mirror-image of the other.

This is partly a matter of translation. The King James and most other versions present us with a Job who, in his last words, "abhor[s] [him]self / and repent[s] in dust and ashes." They do this on the shakiest of philological grounds; though understandably, because they are thinking with orthodox Christian ideas and *expecting* to find penitence and self-abasement as the appropriate response to the righteous, ill-tempered god they expect to find. Nor is this only a Christian mind-set. (For example, the joke about the rabbi who on Yom Kippur walks to the front of his congregation, pounds his chest, and shouts, "I am worthless, Lord, I am worthless." Then the president of the synagogue walks to the front, pounds his chest, and shouts, "I am worthless, Lord, I am worthless." Next, to the surprise and scandal of everyone, the wimpy little beadle walks to the front, pounds his chest, and shouts, "I am worthless, Lord, I am worthless." The rabbi turns to the president and sneers, "Look who's saying he's worthless!")

But self-abasement is just inverted egoism. Anyone who acts with genuine humility will be as far from humiliation as from arrogance. *Wherefore I abhor myself* indeed! How could this poet, after a venture of unprecedented daring, end with a hero merely beaten into submission? Thereby proving that the friends' degraded opinion is correct after all, since Job, by acknowledging that he is a vermin among vermin, acknowledges the god who mistrusts his angels and in whose nose heaven stinks.

Job's response will not accommodate such whimpering. He has received his answer, and can only remain awe-stricken in the face of overwhelming beauty and dread. At Alamogordo on July 16, 1945, Robert Oppenheimer responded to another kind of vision by remembering a verse from the *Bhagavad Gita*: "I [God] am death, the shatterer of worlds." And indeed, the only scriptural analogy to God's answer (the other Biblical examples, except for the burning bush, are of a lesser god) is the vision granted to Arjuna in chapter 11 of the *Gita*, in which that prince experiences, down to the marrow of his bones, the glory and the terror of the universe, all creation and all destruction, embraced in the blissful play of the Supreme Lord. The manifestations there are more cosmic than in *Job*, and the realization of God as "the Self seated in the heart of all creatures" is far clearer. But Job's vision is the more vivid, I think, because its imagination is so deeply rooted in the things of this world. Reading the two together, we are likely to feel even more powerfully the earthliness that moved the author of *Job* to write in such magnificent, loving detail of the lioness and the wild ass and the horse, those creatures as radiant in their pure being as the light that is "brighter than a thousand suns."

Job's final words issue from surrender; not from submission, which even at its purest, in the "Naked I came . . ." of the prologue, is a gesture in a power transaction, between slave and master or defeated and conqueror, and is always a mode of spiritual depression. Surrender, on the contrary, means the wholehearted giving-up of oneself. It is both the ultimate generosity and the ultimate poverty, because in it the giver becomes the gift. When Job says, "I had heard of you with my ears; / but now my eyes have seen you," he is no longer a servant, who fears god and avoids evil. He has faced evil, has looked straight into its face and through it, into a vast wonder and love.

Instead of bursting into fervid adoration as Arjuna does, Job remains a hairsbreadth away from silence. His words are a miracle of tact. We are not told the details of his realization; that isn't necessary; everything is present in the serenity of his tone. All we know is that his grief and accusations, his ideas about God and pity for man, arose from utter ignorance. But we can intuit more than that. A man who hungers and thirsts after justice is not satisfied with a menu. It is not enough for him to hope or believe or know that there is absolute justice in the universe: he must taste and see it. It is not enough that there may be justice someday in the golden haze of the future: it must be now; must *always* have been now.

From this point of vision, the idea that there are accidents or victims is an optical illusion. This statement may seem cruel. Certainly it is a difficult statement. How could it not be? Paradise isn't handed out like a piece of cake at a Sunday school picnic. But the statement is not cruel. It is the opposite of cruel. Once the personal will is surrendered, future and past disappear, the morning stars burst out singing, and the deep will, contemplating the world it has created, says, "Behold, it is very good."

Job's comfort at the end is in his mortality. The physical body is acknowledged as dust, the personal drama as delusion. It is as if the world we perceive through our senses, that whole gorgeous and terrible pageant, were the breath-thin surface of a bubble, and everything else, inside and outside, is pure radiance. Both suffering and joy come then like a brief reflection, and death like a pin.

He feels he has woken up from a dream. That sense, of actually seeing the beloved reality he has only heard of before, is what makes his emotion at the end so convincing. He has let go of everything, and surrendered into the light.

## VI

And there, beyond words, the poem ends. But the author added a prose epilogue, since stories need to be finished, and fairy tales want to end happily ever after. This epilogue has upset and offended many modern readers. "How," they ask, "can Job bear to enter a new life after all the agony he has been put through? And how can he accept brand-new children as a replacement for his murdered sons and daughters? What a mockery!"

We need to realize, though, that the author has changed language again, and thereby changed realities. We have descended to the smaller humanity of the old legend. Here the new children *are* the old children: even though Job's possessions are doubled, he is given seven sons and three daughters, as before, all of them instantaneously grown up; they have sprung back to life as gracefully as the bones of a murdered child in a Grimms' tale. On another level, all the possessions, and the children too, are outer and visible signs of Job's inner fulfillment, present beyond gain and loss. ("The Messiah will come," Kafka said, "only when he is no longer necessary.") Job's anxiety has vanished. Even his god, though he still cares about burnt offerings and ritual expiation, is not split into a Lord and an Accuser, and no longer needs to administer loyalty tests. Indeed, he rewards Job for having said that the righteous aren't rewarded, and mildly punishes the friends for maintaining that the wicked are punished.

Blake, who with all his gnostic eccentricities is still the only interpreter to understand that the theme of this book is spiritual transformation, makes a clear distinction between the worlds of the prologue and of the epilogue. In his first illustration to *Job*, he draws the patriarch and his wife seated at evening prayer, with Bibles open on their laps, their children kneeling around them; the sheep are drowsing, the dogs are drowsing, they themselves look up to heaven in drowsy piety, with all their musical instruments hanging silent on the central tree. The last engraving, however, shows a world trans-figured: it is sunrise, the whole family is standing up, bright-eyed, each exuberantly playing his or her favorite instrument.

The most curious detail in the epilogue is the mention of Job's daughters. In this new world they are not inferior to their brothers and do not have to go to *their* houses for the annual celebration. Indeed, they are dignified equally by being given a share of Job's wealth as their inheritance. Each is named, while the seven sons remain anonymous. The names themselves—Dove, Cinnamon, and Eye-shadow—symbolize peace, abundance, and a specifically female kind of grace. The story's center of gravity has shifted from righteousness to beauty, the effortless manifestation of inner peace. "And in all the world there were no women as beautiful as Job's daughters."

There is something enormously satisfying about this prominence of the feminine at the end of *Job.* The whole yin side of humanity, denigrated in the figure of Job's wife, and in Job's great oath looked upon as a seductive danger, has finally been acknowledged and honored here. It is as if, once Job has learned to surrender, his world too gives up the male compulsion to control. The daughters have almost the last word. They appear with the luminous power of figures in a dream: we can't quite figure out why they are so important, but we know that they are.

The very last word is a peaceful death in the midst of a loving family. What truer, happier ending could there be?

## NOTES TO INTRODUCTION

p. vii, *its hero is a Gentile:* Job is one of the *b'nay qedem,* literally "sons of the east" (1:3), and a native of the land of Uz.

The sons of the east are mentioned in the Book of Judges along with other non-Israelite tribes in or bordering on the land of Canaan: "And it happened, when Israel had sown, that the Midianites attacked, and the Amalekites, and the sons of the east attacked also" (Jg. 6:3; also 6:33, 7:12, 8:10; cf. Gen. 25:6, 19:1, Is. 11:14, Ez. 25:4,10). A later reference in First Kings seems to be a more general usage of the phrase: "And Solomon's wisdom surpassed the wisdom of the sons of the east and all the wisdom of Egypt" (1 Kings 5:10). In either sense, the sons of the east are certainly Gentiles.

As for the land of Uz, there are two conflicting traditions. The first is based on Gen. 10:23 and places it in northern Mesopotamia or the Hauran. The second identifies it with Edom, to the southeast of Canaan. The relevant Biblical verses are: "Rejoice and be glad, O daughter of Edom, who livest in the land of Uz . . ." (Lam. 4:21); "And all the mingled people, and all the kings of the land of Uz, and all the kings of the land of the Philistines, and Ashkelon, and Azzah, and Ekron, and the remnant of Ashdod" (Jer. 25:20). For an exhaustive survey of the evidence, see Dhorme, *The Book of Job,* pp. xxi ff.

p. vii, *Its author may have been as well:* The language of *Job* is so idiosyncratic and contains so many "Arabisms" and "Aramaisms" that some scholars have postulated a lost original text, of which the Hebrew text is a translation. This was also the opinion of Abraham Ibn Ezra, the great medieval rabbinic commentator.

p. viii, *a legend that was already ancient:* Scholars have placed *Job* anywhere between 800 and 300 B.C.E. There are Sumerian versions of the legend dating from 2000 B.C.E.

p. viii, *something so servile:* "My servant Job" can also, in Hebrew, mean "my slave Job."

p. xiv, *"If the wrong man . . .":* From *The Recorded Dialogues of Ch'an Master Chao-chou Ts'ung-shen.*

p. xiv, *the text itself becomes defective:* In the Massoretic (traditional Hebrew) text, Bildad's last speech, for example, contains only five verses, and Zophar's is missing entirely.

p. xxiv, *Second Isaiah:* Is. 45:7.

p. xxv, *on the shakiest of philological grounds:* The first verb, *'em'as,* means "to reject" or "to regard as of little value," never "to abhor or despise." Since the object has somehow dropped out of the Massoretic text, it must be supplied by the translator. "Myself" is based on a misunderstanding of the verb. A sounder interpretation, first proposed in the ancient Syriac version, would be: "Therefore I take back [everything I said]."

In the second half of the verse, the verb, as used in *Job,* always means "to comfort." The phrase *nihamti 'al* means "to be comforted about" or possibly "to repent of," but not "to repent in or upon." Nor does *'afar va-'efer* indicate the place where Job is sitting. This phrase, which occurs once before in *Job* and twice elsewhere in the Bible, always refers to the human body, which was created from dust and returns to dust. So the literal meaning is: "and I am comforted about [being] dust."

# The Book of JOB

PROLOGUE:
# The Legend

Once upon a time, in the land of Uz, there was a man named Job. He was a man of perfect integrity, who feared God and avoided evil. He had seven sons and three daughters; seven thousand sheep, three thousand camels, five hundred yoke of oxen, and five hundred donkeys; and also many slaves. He was the richest man in the East.

Every year, his sons would hold a great banquet, in the house of each of them in turn, and they would invite their sisters to come feast with them. When the week of celebration was over, Job would have them come to be purified; for he thought, "Perhaps my children have sinned, and cursed God in their hearts." Job did this every year.

One year, on the day when the angels come to testify before the Lord, the Accusing Angel came too.

The Lord said to the Accuser, "Where have you come from?"

The Accuser answered, "From walking here and there on the earth, and looking around."

The Lord said, "Did you notice my servant Job? There is no one on earth like him: a man of perfect integrity, who fears God and avoids evil."

The Accuser said, "Doesn't Job have a good reason for being so good? Haven't you put a hedge around him—himself and his whole family and everything he has? You bless whatever he does, and the land is teeming with his cattle. But just reach out and strike everything he has, and I bet he'll curse you to your face."

The Lord said, "All right: everything he has is in your power. Just don't lay a hand on him."

Then the Accuser left.

That same day, as Job's sons and daughters were feasting in the house of the eldest brother, a messenger came to Job and said, "The oxen were plowing and the donkeys grazing and the Sabeans attacked and took them and killed the boys and only I escaped to tell you." Before he had finished speaking, another one came and said, "Lightning fell from the sky and burned up the sheep and boys and only I escaped to tell you." Before he had finished speaking, another one came and said, "Chaldeans attacked the camels and took them and killed the boys and only I escaped to tell you." Before he had finished speaking, another one came and said, "Your sons and daughters were feasting and a great wind came out of the desert and knocked down the walls of the house and it fell on them and they're dead and only I escaped to tell you."

Then Job stood up. He tore his robe. He shaved his head. He lay down with his face in the dust. He said, "Naked I came from my mother's womb, and naked I will return there. The Lord gave, and the Lord has taken; may the name of the Lord be blessed."

Once again, on the day when the angels come to testify before the Lord, the Accusing Angel came too.

The Lord said to the Accuser, "Where have you come from?"

The Accuser answered, "From walking here and there on the earth, and looking around."

The Lord said, "Did you notice my servant Job? There is no one on earth like him: a man of perfect integrity, who fears God and avoids evil. He is holding on to his innocence, even after you made me torment him for no reason."

The Accuser said, "So what? A man will give up everything he has, to save his own skin. But just reach out and strike his flesh and bones, and I bet he'll curse you to your face."

The Lord said, "All right: he is in your power. Just don't kill him."

Then the Accuser left.

He covered Job with boils, from his scalp to the soles of his feet. Job took a piece of broken pottery to scratch himself with, and sat down in the dust.

His wife said to him, "How long will you go on clinging to your innocence? Curse God, and die."

Job said, "Foolish woman, have you lost your mind? We have accepted good fortune from God; surely we can accept bad fortune too."

Now Job had three friends—Eliphaz the Temanite, Bildad the Shuhite, and Zophar the Namathite. When these friends heard of all the calamities that had come upon him, each of them left his own country to mourn with Job and to comfort him. They met at an appointed place and went on together. When they arrived and saw Job from a distance, they could barely recognize him. They cried out, and tore their clothing, and sprinkled dust on their heads. Then they sat with him for seven days and seven nights. And no one said a word, for they saw how great his suffering was.

# The Curse

FINALLY JOB CRIED OUT:

God damn the day I was born
    and the night that forced me from the womb.
On that day—let there be darkness;
    let it never have been created;
    let it sink back into the void.
Let chaos overpower it;
    let black clouds overwhelm it;
    let the sun be plucked from its sky.
Let oblivion overshadow it;
    let the other days disown it;
    let the aeons swallow it up.
On that night—let no child be born,
    no mother cry out with joy.
Let sorcerers wake the Serpent
    to blast it with eternal blight.
Let its last stars be extinguished;
    let it wait in terror for daylight;
    let its dawn never arrive.
For it did not shut the womb's doors
    to shelter me from this sorrow.

Why couldn't I have died
    as they pulled me out of the dark?
Why were there knees to hold me,
    breasts to keep me alive?
If only I had strangled or drowned
    on my way to the bitter light.

Now I would be at rest,
    I would be sound asleep,
with kings and lords of the earth
    who lived in echoing halls,
with princes who hoarded silver
    and filled their cellars with gold.
There the troubled are calm;
    there the exhausted rest.
Rich and poor are alike there,
    and the slave lies next to his master.

Why is there light for the wretched,
    life for the bitter-hearted,
who long for death, who seek it
    as if it were buried treasure,
who smile when they reach the graveyard
    and laugh as their pit is dug.
For God has hidden my way
    and put hedges across my path.
I sit and gnaw on my grief;
    my groans pour out like water.
My worst fears have happened;
    my nightmares have come to life.
Silence and peace have abandoned me,
    and anguish camps in my heart.

# The First Round

THEN ELIPHAZ THE TEMANITE SAID:

These words will perhaps upset you;
    but I cannot hold back my thoughts.
Once you encouraged the timid
    and filled the frightened with strength.
You brought relief to the comfortless,
    gave the desperate hope.
But now it is *your* turn, you tremble;
    now *you* are the victim, you shudder.

Have you lost all faith in your piety,
    all hope in your perfect conduct?
Can an innocent man be punished?
    Can a good man die in distress?
I have seen the plowers of evil
    reaping the crimes they sowed.
One breath from God and they shrivel up;
    one blast of his rage and they burn.
The lion may roar with fury,
    but his teeth are cracked in his mouth.
The jackal howls and goes hungry;
    the wolf is driven away.

Now a word, in secret, came to me,
    a whisper crept in my ear,
at night, when visions flash
    and ecstasy grips the mind.

Terror caught me; panic
    shook my bones like sticks.
Something breathed on my face;
    my hair stood stiff.
I could barely see—a spirit—
    hovering on my chest—
a soft voice, speaking:
*How can man be righteous?*
    *How can mortals be pure?*
*If God distrusts his own servants*
    *and charges the angels with sin,*
*what of those who are built of clay*
    *and live in bodies of dust?*
*They are snapped like bits of straw;*
    *their lives are blown out like candles . . .*
    *they vanish, and who can save them?*

Call now: will anyone answer?
    To which of the angels will you turn?
For anger destroys the fool,
    and passion flays the ignorant.
I have seen the fool rooted up,
    his house collapsing in ruins,
his children stripped naked
    with no one to help or pity them,
the hungry devouring his harvest,
    the thirsty gulping his wine.
For pain does not spring from the dust
    or sorrow sprout from the soil:
man is the father of sorrow,
    as surely as sparks fly upward.

If I were you, I would pray;
    I would put my case before God.
His workings are vast and fathomless,
    his wonders beyond our grasp.
He lifts up the despised
    and leads the abandoned to safety.
He traps the wise in their cleverness
    and ruins the plots of the cunning.
By day they stumble in shadows;
    at noon they grope in the dark.
But he plucks the poor from danger
    and the meek from the power of wrong.
Then there is hope for the wretched,
    and wickedness shuts its mouth.

You are lucky that God has scolded you;
    so take his lesson to heart.
For he wounds, but then binds up;
    he injures, but then he heals.
When disaster strikes, he will rescue you
    and never let evil touch you.
In war he will save you from bloodshed,
    in famine from the grip of death.
When slander roams he will hide you;
    you will laugh in calamity's face.
In league with the stones of the field,
    in concord with savage beasts,
you will know that your house is protected
    and your meadows safe from harm.
You will see your family multiply,
    your children flourish like grass.

You will die at the height of your powers
and be gathered like ripened grain.

I know that these things are true:
consider them now, and learn.

THEN JOB SAID:

If ever my grief were measured
    or my sorrow put on a scale,
it would outweigh the sands of the ocean:
    that is why I am desperate.
For God has ringed me with terrors,
    and his arrows have pierced my heart.
When a donkey has grass, does he bray?
    Does an ox low near his fodder?
Can gruel be eaten unsalted?
    Is there taste in the white of an egg?
My lips refuse to touch it;
    my heart is sickened at its sight.

If only my prayer were answered
    and God granted my wish.
If only he made an end of me,
    snipping my life like a thread.
That is my only comfort
    as I writhe in this savage pain.
How long can I keep on waiting?
    Why should I stay alive?
Is my body hard as a rock?
    Is my flesh made of brass?
All my strength has left me;
    all hope has been driven away.

My friends are streams that go dry,
    riverbeds in the desert.
In spring they are dark with ice,
    swollen with melted snow.
But when summer comes they are gone;
    they vanish in the blazing heat.
Pilgrims search for them everywhere
    and lose their way in the dust.
They wander dazed, panting;
    their tongues parch and turn black.

You too have turned against me;
    my wretchedness fills you with fear.
Have I ever asked you to help me
    or begged you to pay my ransom,
to rescue me from an enemy
    or save me from an oppressor?
Teach me, and I will be silent;
    show me where I am wrong.
Does honest speech offend you?
    Are you shocked by what I have said?
Do you want to disprove my passion
    or argue away my despair?
Look me straight in the eye:
    is this how a liar would face you?
Can't I tell right from wrong?
    If I sinned, wouldn't I know it?

Man's life is a prison;
    he is sentenced to pain and grief.
Like a slave he pants for the shadows;
    like a servant he longs for rest.
Each day I live seems endless,
    and I suffer through endless nights.
When I lie down, I long for morning;
    when I get up, I long for evening;
    all day I toss and turn.
My flesh crawls with maggots;
    my skin cracks and oozes.
My days fly past me like a shuttle,
    and my hope snaps like a thread.

Remember: life is a breath;
    soon I will vanish from your sight.
The eye that looks will not see me;
    you may search, but I will be gone.
Like a cloud fading in the sky,
    man dissolves into death.
He leaves the whole world behind him
    and never comes home again.

Therefore I refuse to be quiet;
    I will cry out my bitter despair.
Am I the Sea or the Serpent,
    that you pen me behind a wall?

If I say, "Sleep will comfort me,
    I will lie down to ease my pain,"
then you terrify me with visions,
    your nightmares choke me with horror,
and I wake up gasping for breath,
    longing to be dead at last.
I will not live forever;
    leave me, for my days are wind.

What is man, that you notice him,
    turn your glare upon him,
examine him every morning,
    test him at every instant?
Won't you even give me
    time to swallow my spit?
If I sinned, what have I done
    to you, Watcher of Men?
Why have you made me your target
    and burdened me with myself?
Can't you forgive my sins
    or overlook my mistakes?
For soon I will lie in the dust;
    you will call, but I will be gone.

**THEN BILDAD THE SHUHITE SAID:**

How long will you go on ranting,
    filling our ears with trash?
Does God make straightness crooked
    or turn truth upside down?
Your children must have been evil:
    he punished them for their crimes.
But if you are pure and righteous
    and pray to God for mercy,
surely he will answer your prayer
    and fulfill your greatest desires.
Your past will seem like a trifle,
    so blessed will your future be.

Go learn from the wisdom of the ages;
    listen to the patriarchs' words.
For we are small and ignorant;
    our days on earth are a shadow.
But their advice will guide you,
    and their answers will give you peace.

Can papyrus grow without water?
    Can a reed flourish in sand?
As crisp and fresh as it looked,
    it wilts like a blade of grass.
Such is the fate of the impious,
    the empty hope of the sinner.

His peace of mind is gossamer;
    his faith is a spider's web.
Though he props up his house, it collapses;
    though he builds it again, it falls.

But the righteous blossom in sunlight,
    and the garden is filled with their seeds.
Their roots twine around stones
    and fasten even to rocks.
If they are plucked from the ground,
    rooted up from their soil,
they rejoice wherever they go
    and bloom again from the dust.

God never betrays the innocent
    or takes the hand of the wicked.
He will yet fill your mouth with laughter,
    and joy will burst from your lips.
Your enemies will drown in their shame,
    and the wind will blow through their houses.

THEN JOB SAID:

I know that this is true:
    no man can argue with God
or answer even one
    of a thousand accusations.
However wise or powerful—
    who could oppose him and live?
He levels cliffs in an instant,
    rooting them up in his rage;
he knocks the earth from its platform
    and shakes the pillars of the sky;
he talks to the sun—it darkens;
    he clamps a seal on the stars.
He alone stretched out the heavens
    and trampled the heights of the sea;
he made the Bear and the Hunter,
    the Scorpion, the Twins.
His workings are vast and fathomless,
    his wonders beyond my grasp.
If he passed me, I would not see him;
    if he went by, I would not know.
If he seized me, who could stop him
    or cry out, "What are you doing?"
He will never hold back his fury;
    the Dragon lies at his feet.

How then can *I* refute him
> or marshal my words against him?
How can I prove my innocence?
> Do I have to beg him for mercy?
If I testify, will he answer?
> Is he listening to my plea?
He has punished me for a trifle;
> for no reason he gashes my flesh.
He makes me gasp with terror;
> he plunges me into despair.
For in strength, he is far beyond me;
> and in eloquence, who is like him?
I am guiltless, but his mouth condemns me;
> blameless, but his words convict me.
He does not care; so I say
> he murders both the pure and the wicked.
When the plague brings sudden death,
> he laughs at the anguish of the innocent.
He hands the earth to the wicked
> and blindfolds its judges' eyes.
> Who does it, if not he?

My days sprint past me like runners;
> I will never see them again.
They glide by me like sailboats;
> they swoop down like hawks on their prey.
If I want to forget my misery
> or try to smile at my pain,
one thought makes me shudder:
> that you don't believe what I say.

If I am already guilty,
    why should I struggle on?
Should I wash my body in snow,
    scour my face with sand?
You would toss me into a cesspool,
    and my own stench would make me vomit.
If only there were an arbiter
    who could lay his hand on us both,
who could make you put down your club
    and hold back your terrible arm.
Then, without fear, I would say,
    You have not treated me justly.

I loathe each day of my life;
    I will take my complaint to God.
I will say, Do not condemn me;
    why are you so enraged?
Is it right for you to be vicious,
    to spoil what your own hands made?
Are your eyes mere eyes of flesh?
    Is your vision no keener than a man's?
Is your mind like a human mind?
    Are your feelings human feelings?
For you keep pursuing a sin,
    trying to dig up a crime,
though you *know* that I am innocent
    and cannot escape from your grip.

Your hands molded and made me,
    and someday you will destroy me.

Remember: you formed me from clay
    and will soon turn me back to dust.
You poured me out like milk,
    made me curdle like cheese,
clothed me in flesh and skin,
    knit me with bones and sinews.
You loved me, you gave me life,
    you nursed and cared for my spirit.
Yet this you hid in your heart,
    this I know was your purpose:
to watch me, and if ever I sinned
    to punish me for the rest of my days.
You lash me if I am guilty,
    shame me if I am not.
You set me free, then trap me,
    like a cat toying with a mouse.

Why did you let me be born?
    Why couldn't I have stayed
in the deep waters of the womb,
    rocked to sleep in the dark?
Is my life not wretched enough?
    Leave me one moment of peace,
before I must go away
    to the land of endless shadows,
the land of gloom and sighing,
    where dawn is as black as night.

THEN ZOPHAR THE NAMATHITE SAID:

Should this man be saved by his words,
    acquitted because he speaks well?
Should you mouth us into submission
    and go on with your impudent lies?
You say, "My conscience is clear";
    you think that your life is spotless.
But if God were to cross-examine you
    and turned up your hidden motives
and presented his case against you
    and told you why he has punished you—
    you would know that your guilt is great.

How can you understand God
    or fathom his endless wisdom?
It is higher than heaven—can you reach it?,
    deeper than hell—can you touch it?,
wider than all the earth,
    broader than the breadth of the sea.
If he seizes and casts in prison
    and condemns—who can stop him?
For he knows that you are a sinner;
    he sees and judges your crimes.
But a stupid man will be wise
    when a cow gives birth to a zebra.

Come now, repent of your sins;
    open your heart to God.
Wash your hands of their wickedness;
    banish crime from your door.
Then your soul will be pure;
    your heart will be firm and fearless.
All your suffering will vanish,
    flowing away like a stream.
Your life will shine like the sun;
    your darkest day will be bright.
Your faith will be unshakable;
    your mind will be strong and serene.
No one will dare to disturb you;
    many will seek your favor.
But the wicked will all be punished;
    they will live in constant terror;
    their hope will become a noose.

THEN JOB SAID:

You, it seems, know everything;
    perfect wisdom is yours.
But I am not an idiot:
    who does not know such things?
Even the animals will tell you,
    and the birds in the sky will teach you.
Any plant will instruct you;
    go learn from the fish in the sea.
Which of them does not know
    that God created all things?
In his hand is the soul of all beings
    and the spirit of every man.

Doesn't the mind understand
    as simply as the tongue tastes?
Do all men grow in knowledge?
    Are they wise because they are old?
Only God is wise;
    knowledge is his alone.
He tears down—no man can build;
    he imprisons—no man can free.
He holds back the rain—there is drought;
    he pours it—it floods the earth.
Power belongs to him only;
    deceived and deceiver are his.
He turns great lords into morons,
    priests into driveling fools.

He pushes kings off their thrones
    and knocks the crown from their heads.
He strips the wise of their reason
    and makes the eloquent mute.
He pours contempt on princes
    and crushes the high and haughty.
He puffs up nations and wrecks them,
    blotting them out in their pride.
He drives great rulers insane
    and drops them alone in the wilderness.
They grope about in the dark,
    staggering as if they were drunk.

All this I have seen with my own eyes;
    my own ears have heard these things.
What you know, I know also;
    my mind is as clear as yours.
But I want to speak before God,
    to present my case in God's court.
For *you* smear my wounds with ignorance
    and patch my body with lies.
Don't you have any sense?
    Will you never shut your mouths?

Listen now to my arguments;
    hear out my accusations.
Will you lie to vindicate God?
    Will you perjure yourselves for him?
Will you blindly stand on his side,
    pleading his case alone?

What will you do when he questions you?
    Can you cheat him as you would a man?
Won't he judge you severely
    if your testimony is false?
Won't he crush you with terror
    and chill your bones with fear?
Your answers are dusty answers;
    your words crumble like clay.

Be quiet now—let *me* speak;
    whatever happens will happen.
I will take my flesh in my teeth,
    hold my life in my hands.
He may kill me, but I won't stop;
    I will speak the truth, to his face.
Listen now to my words;
    pay attention to what I say.
For I have prepared my defense,
    and I know that I am right.

Grant me one thing only,
    and I will not hide from your face:
do not numb me with fear
    or flood my heart with your terror.
Accuse me—I will respond;
    or let me speak, and answer me.
What crime have I committed?
    How have I sinned against you?
Why do you hide your face
    as if I were your enemy?

Will you frighten a withered leaf
    or hunt down a piece of straw?
For you count up all my errors
    and convict me for the sins of my youth.
You put my legs in shackles;
    you brand the soles of my feet;
    you follow my every step.

Man who is born of woman—
    how few and harsh are his days!
Like a flower he blooms and withers;
    like a shadow he fades in the dark.
He falls apart like a wine-skin,
    like a garment chewed by moths.
And must *you* take notice of *him?*
    Must *you* call *him* to account?
Since all his days are determined
    and the sum of his years is set—
look away; leave him alone;
    grant him peace, for one moment.

Even if it is cut down,
    a tree can return to life.
Though its roots decay in the ground
    and its stump grows old and rotten,
it will bud at the scent of water
    and bloom as if it were young.
But man is cut down forever;
    he dies, and where is he then?

The lake is drained of its water,
    the river becomes a ditch,
and man will not rise again
    while the sky is above the earth.

If only you would hide me in the pit
    till your anger has passed away,
    then come to me and release me.
All my days in prison
    I would sit and wait for that time.
You would call me—I would answer;
    you would come to me and rejoice,
delighting in my smallest step
    like a father watching his child.

But cliffs fall to the ground;
    boulders crumble away;
mountains are turned to dust;
    and you destroy man's hope.
You crush him into the ground,
    send him away disfigured.
If his sons are honored, does he know?
    If his daughters are shamed, does he care?
Only his own flesh hurts him,
    and he mourns for himself alone.

# The Second Round

THEN ELIPHAZ THE TEMANITE SAID:

Does a wise man spout such nonsense
    and fill his belly with gas?
Does he blurt out useless arguments,
    words that can do no good?
You are undermining religion
    and crippling faith in God.
Sin has seduced your mind;
    your tongue flaps with deceit.
Your mouth condemns you, not I;
    your own lips testify against you.

Are you the first man to be born,
    created before the mountains?
Have you listened in at God's keyhole
    and crept away with his plans?
What do you know that *we* don't?
    What have you seen that we haven't?
We are old; our beards are white;
    we speak with the wisdom of age.
Will you scorn religion's comforts
    and reject our indulgent advice?
What has taken hold of you?
    What has made you so wild
that you spew your anger at God
    and spit out such insolent words?

What is man—is he pure?
> Can a son of woman be sinless?
If God mistrusts his angels
> and heaven stinks in his nose,
what of that vermin, man,
> who laps up filth like water?

Listen now to my words;
> I will tell you what I have seen—
what the sages too have said
> and the wise have never kept hidden:
The wicked man's life is a torment;
> his days are anguish and pain.
In his ear is the voice of terror;
> in his mouth is the taste of death.
He flees from darkness to darkness;
> he is marked for the edge of the sword.
His body is food for vultures;
> disaster nibbles his flesh.
Anguish pounds at his mind;
> fear and panic assault him,
> like a soldier before a battle.

For he shook his fist at God
> and dared to revolt against him,
charging at him headlong
> behind the spikes of his shield.
Though his face was plump and cheerful
> and his thighs bulged with health,

he lives in a desolate city
    and sleeps in an empty room.
All his works have decayed;
    his roots have rotted in the ground.
The sun withered his shoots;
    his blossoms fell in the wind.
His leaves shriveled and died;
    all his branches are bare.
He was stripped of his grapes like a vine
    and dropped his buds like an olive tree.

For the fate of the wicked is barren,
    and his hopes are consumed by fire.
His womb is heavy with suffering;
    he gives birth to sorrow and pain.

**THEN JOB SAID:**

Enough—I have heard enough!
    I am sick of your consolations!
How long will you pelt me with insults?
    Will your malice never relent?
I too could say such things
    if you were in my position:
I could bury you with accusations
    and sneer at you in my piety;
or whisper my easy comfort
    and encourage you with a word.

But I speak, and my pain keeps raging;
    I am silent, and have no relief.
For disaster has worn me out,
    and suffering has made me wither.
In his rage he hunted and caught me;
    he cracked my bones in his teeth.
I was whole—he ripped me apart,
    chewed my body to pulp.
He set me up as a target;
    his arrows tore through my flesh.
He hacked my liver to pieces;
    he poured my gall on the ground.
He besieged me like a fortress;
    he demolished my inmost walls.

I have wrapped my skin in sackcloth
　　and laid my head in the dust.
My face is swollen from weeping;
　　shadows circle my eyes—
although my hands are spotless
　　and the prayer of my heart is pure.

O Earth, do not cover my blood!
　　Never let my cry be buried!
For I have a witness in heaven,
　　a spokesman above the clouds.
May he judge between mortal and God
　　as he would between man and neighbor.
For grief has darkened my eyes;
　　my body is like a shadow.
My days fade like an echo;
　　the strings of my heart have snapped.
And soon my life will vanish;
　　I will walk down into the dust.

I have taken the pit as my home
　　and made my bed in the dark.
I have called the grave my father;
　　the worm my mother, my sister.
And where now is my hope?
　　My piety—who will see it?
It will follow me to the grave
　　and lie in the dust beside me.

**THEN BILDAD THE SHUHITE SAID:**

How long will you lay these word-snares?
    Be sensible: then we will talk.
Why do you treat us like morons
    and act as if we were cows?
Should the earth be changed for *your* sake
    and mountains move at your bidding?

It is true: the sinner is snuffed out;
    his candle flickers and dies.
His arrogant steps are hobbled;
    he is tripped by his own deceit.
A net catches his legs;
    he stumbles into a pit.
His heels stick in a trap;
    a noose snaps his neck.
The terrors of death surround him
    and make him piss in his pants.
Misfortune hungers after him;
    disaster waits at his side.
Sickness gnaws his flesh;
    death picks his bones.
Fire guts his house;
    sulphur rains on his fields.
All his roots are withered;
    all his branches are bare.

He disappears from the earth;
    not a trace is left behind him.
He is thrown into endless darkness
    and locked out of the world.
At his fate the East is appalled,
    and terror grips the West.

This is what happens to the godless;
    this is the sinner's doom.

THEN JOB SAID:

How long will you make me suffer
    and crush my heart with your words?
Again and again you mock me
    and wrong me with shameless lies.
Do you think I have lost my mind?
    Am *I* the one who is raving?
Are you sure that you have convicted me
    and justified my disgrace?

No—because God has tricked me,
    and lured me into his trap.
I call, but there is no answer;
    I cry out, and where is justice?
He made my road impassable,
    covered my path with darkness,
stripped me of my honor,
    knocked the crown from my head.
He broke me, rooted me up,
    left me in little pieces.
His anger set me on fire;
    his hatred burned me to ashes.

All my friends have forgotten me;
    my neighbors have thrown me away.
My relatives look through me
    as though I didn't exist.

My servants refuse to hear me;
    they shun me like a leper.
My breath sickens my wife;
    my stench disgusts my brothers.
Even young children fear me;
    when they see me, they run away.
My dearest friends despise me;
    I have lost everyone I love.
Have pity on me, my friends,
    for God's fist has struck me.
Why must you hunt me as God does?
    Why do you gnaw my flesh?

If only my cry were recorded
    and my plea inscribed on a tablet—
carved with an iron stylus,
    chiseled in rock forever.
Someday my witness would come;
    my avenger would read those words.
He would plead for me in God's court;
    he would stand up and vindicate my name.

THEN ZOPHAR THE NAMATHITE SAID:

My mind is seething with anger,
    and rage drives me to speak.
I have heard enough of your insults;
    you answer our wisdom with lies.

Haven't you realized yet
    (How can you be so blind!)
that the sinner's joy is brief
    and lasts no more than a moment?
Though he rises as high as heaven
    and his forehead touches the clouds,
he will drop to the ground like dung
    and rot like a fallen fruit.
He flies away like a vision,
    vanishes like a dream.
His friends do not give him a thought;
    his children forget his name.
His body may pulse with vigor,
    but soon he will lie in the dust.

Though crime was sweet on his lips
    and evil melted in his mouth,
though he tried to keep its flavor
    and hold its taste on his tongue,
the food that he swallowed turns
    to poison inside his belly.

He chews the head of a viper,
	sucks the tongue of a snake.
He loses his vats of oil;
	his cream and honey are spilled.
He is forced to spit up his riches
	and vomit out all his wealth.

For he crushed the weak and the helpless;
	he pushed the poor from their huts.
His hunger gave him no rest;
	he was driven by his desire;
nothing escaped his greed:
	therefore his wealth will vanish.
At the height of his fortune he falls;
	every disaster strikes him.
The wrath of God assaults him;
	calamities rain on his head.
Total darkness engulfs him;
	fire from heaven consumes him.
Storms demolish his fields;
	floods sweep away his house.
Heaven reveals his guilt,
	and earth rises against him.

This is the fate of the sinner;
	this is the rebel's reward.

**THEN JOB SAID:**

Listen now to my words;
    let that be the comfort you give me.
Bear with me: let me speak;
    when I finish, then you can laugh.
Is my grievance against a man?
    Why shouldn't I be impatient?
Look at me: be appalled;
    clap your hands to your mouths.
When I think of it I am terrified
    and horror chills my flesh.

Why do the wicked prosper
    and live to a ripe old age?
Their children stand beside them;
    their grandchildren sit on their laps.
Their houses are safe from danger,
    secure from the wrath of God.
Not one of their bulls is impotent;
    not one of their cows miscarries.
Their grandchildren run out to play,
    skipping about like lambs,
singing to drum and lyre,
    dancing to the sound of the flute.
They end their lives in prosperity
    and go to the grave in peace.

Yet they tell God, "Leave us alone;
    we can't be bothered about you.
Why should we pray to God?
    What good will it do us to serve you?"

Is the lamp of the sinner snuffed out?
    Does misfortune knock on his door?
Is he really driven like chaff,
    blown like straw in the wind?
Is calamity saved for his children?
    Let him have his punishment *now!*
Let his own eyes see disaster!
    Let him choke on the wrath of God!
For what does he care about others
    when his own life comes to an end?

One man dies serenely,
    lapped in safety and comfort,
his thighs bulging with fat,
    the marrow moist in his bones.
Another dies in despair,
    his life bitter on his tongue.
But both men rot in the ground,
    and maggots chew on them both.

I know what you are thinking,
    the lies you have slapped together.
You say, "But where is the rich man?
    Show us the homes of the wicked!"

Haven't you talked with travelers?
    Don't you know from their tales
that the sinner escapes destruction
    and is spared on the day of wrath?
No one condemns his sins
    or punishes him for his crimes.
He is carried with pomp to the graveyard;
    thousands weep by his coffin.
He is tucked into the earth,
    and flowers bloom on his grave.

How hollow then is your comfort!
    Your answers are empty lies.

# The Third Round

THEN ELIPHAZ THE TEMANITE SAID:

What use can man be to God—
    even the wisest of men?
Does God profit from your goodness
    or gain by your perfect conduct?
Would he sentence you for your piety
    or punish you for your faith?

Your guilt must be great indeed;
    your crimes must be inconceivable.
You cheated your dearest friends,
    stripped your debtors naked,
stole food from the hungry,
    let the destitute starve,
spat on widow and orphan,
    laughed in the beggar's face.
That is why pain surrounds you
    and sudden terror has struck you.
Light is turned to darkness,
    and the waves close over your head.

Since God is far up in heaven,
    higher than the highest stars,
you thought, "What does *he* know?
    Can he see through the thicket of clouds?
How can he judge my actions,
    as he walks on the rim of the sky?"

Why do you keep on sinning,
    as the wicked have always done?
They were cut off before their time;
    they were swept away in a flood.
For they told God, "Leave us alone;
    don't meddle in our affairs."
The righteous saw and were happy;
    the innocent laughed at their fall.
Everything they had was destroyed,
    and all their riches vanished.

Come now: make peace with God;
    make peace: you will not be sorry.
Listen to his instructions;
    keep his words in your heart.
If you humble yourself before him
    and banish sin from your house,
treating your gold like dust,
    your silver like worthless pebbles,
then God will become your treasure,
    more precious than the finest gold.
For then you will trust in God
    and look to heaven for help.
You will pray, and he will hear you;
    he will grant whatever you wish.
Everything you do will succeed,
    and light will shine on your path.
For he does not abandon the innocent;
    if you are pure, he will save you.

THEN JOB SAID:

Still my condition is desperate;
    his fist still beats on my skull.
If only I knew where to meet him
    and could find my way to his court.
I would argue my case before him;
    words would flow from my mouth.
I would counter all his arguments
    and disprove his accusations.
Would he try to overpower me
    or refuse to hear my defense?
Surely he would listen to reason;
    I would surely win my case.
For he knows that I am innocent;
    if he sifts me I will shine like gold.
My feet have walked on his way
    and never strayed from his path.
I have kept all his commandments,
    treasuring his words in my heart.

But he wills, and who can stop him?
    What he wishes to do, he does.
He will go ahead with his plans,
    devising my endless torment.
That is why terror grips me;
    when I think of it, I am appalled.

He has wrung the strength from my mind
    and pumped my heart full with sorrow.
Yet I am not silenced by darkness
    or the night that covers my face.

Where are the days of judgment,
    the times when the wicked are tried?
They steal land from their neighbors
    and walk away with their flocks.
They drive off the orphan's donkey,
    impound the widow's bull.
They push the weak from the pathway
    and force the wretched to hide.

The poor, like herds of cattle,
    wander across the plains,
searching all day for food,
    picking up scraps for their children.
Naked, without a refuge,
    they shiver in the bitter cold.
When it rains, they are drenched to the bone;
    they huddle together in caves.
They carry grain for the wicked
    and break their backs for the rich.
They press olives and starve,
    crush grapes and go thirsty.

In the city the dying groan
    and the wounded cry out for help;
    but God sees nothing wrong.

At twilight the killer appears,
    stalking his helpless victim.
The rapist waits for evening
    and roams through the darkened streets.
The thief crawls from the shadows
    with a hood pulled over his face.
They shut themselves in by day
    and hate the sight of the sun.
Midnight to them is morning;
    they thrive in the terrors of night.

THEN BILDAD THE SHUHITE SAID:

How can a man be pure
    or a son of woman be sinless?
If God despises the moon
    and thinks that the stars are tainted,
what about man, that worm,
    that vile, stinking maggot?

Power belongs to God,
    who makes peace in heaven.
Can his vast battalions be numbered?
    Who can escape his onslaught?
The dead tremble beneath him;
    demons shudder at his name.
The pit is naked before him;
    below him the grave gapes wide.
He stretched the sky over chaos;
    he hung the earth in the void.
He wrapped the waters in rainclouds,
    and they did not burst from the weight.
He set the horizon there,
    at the boundary of light and darkness.
The pillars of heaven trembled;
    the mountains shook at his rage.
With his power he bound the Sea;
    with his cunning he crushed the Dragon.

He shattered the Ocean with his breath
    and pierced the primeval Serpent.

These are the least of his works:
    we hear no more than a whisper;
    for who knows his thunderous might?

**THEN JOB SAID:**

How kind you all have been to me!
    How considerate of my pain!
What would I do without you
    and the good advice you have given?
Who has made you so tactful
    and inspired such compassionate words?

I swear by God, who has wronged me
    and filled my cup with despair,
that while there is life in this body
    and as long as I can breathe,
I will never let you convict me;
    I will never give up my claim.
I will hold tight to my innocence;
    my mind will never submit.

**THEN ZOPHAR THE NAMATHITE SAID:**

What can the sinner hope for
    when God demands his life?
Is he able to trust in God
    and cry out to him at that moment?
Will God be moved by his screaming
    as death takes him by the throat?

This is the sinner's fate,
    the violent man's reward:
Famine devours his daughters;
    his sons are murdered by thieves.
He may heap up silver like dirt,
    pile up the finest linen,
but the righteous inherit his wealth
    and the innocent share his possessions.
His house is frail as a bird's nest,
    weak as a watchman's hut.
He goes to sleep a rich man;
    when he wakes up, his room is bare.
Waves of terror flood over him;
    panic sweeps him away.
The east wind flings itself on him,
    whirls him out of his bed,
claps its hands around him
    and whistles him off in the dark.

# The Summation

THEN JOB SAID:

If only I could return
    to the days when God was my guardian;
when his fire blazed above me
    and guided me through the dark—
to the days when I was in blossom
    and God was a hedge around me;
when he hadn't yet deserted me
    and my children sat at my side;
when my feet were bathed in cream
    and oil gushed from the rock.

As I walked to the square of the city
    and took my seat of honor,
young men held their breath;
    old men rose to their feet;
rich men stopped speaking
    and put their fingers to their lips;
men of authority shuddered,
    and their tongues stuck in their throats.

They listened to me in silence;
    they clung to each of my words.
When I finished, they could not speak,
    for my wisdom had showered upon them.
They thirsted for my speech like rain
    and drank it as if they were dust.

My smile gave them courage;
    my radiant face inspired them.
I sat before them in majesty,
    like a king at the head of his troops.

All ears were filled with my praise;
    every eye was my witness.
For I rescued the poor, the desperate,
    those who had nowhere to turn.
I brought relief to the beggar
    and joy to the widow's heart.
Righteousness was my clothing,
    justice my robe and turban.
I served as eyes for the blind,
    hands and feet for the crippled.
To the destitute I was a father;
    I fought for the stranger's rights.
I broke the jaws of the wicked,
    plucked the spoil from their teeth.
And I thought, "I will live many years,
    growing as old as the palm tree.
My roots will be spread for water,
    and the dew will rest on my boughs."

And now I am jeered at by streetboys,
    whose fathers I would have considered
    unfit to take care of my dogs.
What were *they* but mongrels?
    No one would have called them men.

Shriveled up with hunger,
    they gnawed the desolate wasteland.
They picked leaves for their supper,
    fed on branches and roots.
They were driven out from the cities,
    shouted after like thieves,
to live out their days in the wilderness,
    in caverns or under rocks.
They grunted together in the bushes
    and copulated in the dust—
these misbegotten wretches,
    these outcasts from the land of men.

And now I am their fool;
    they snigger behind my back.
They stand beside me and sneer;
    they walk up and spit in my face.
When they see me, frenzy takes them;
    they turn into savage beasts.
They rush at me in a mob;
    they raise siege-ramps against me.
They tear down my defenses;
    they swarm over my wall.
They burst in at the breach
    and come pouring through like a flood.
Terror rises before me;
    my courage is blown like the wind;
    like a cloud my hope is gone.

And now I am in agony;
>    the days of sorrow have caught me.
Pain pierces my skin;
>    suffering gnaws my bones.
Despair grips me by the neck,
>    shakes me by the collar of my coat.
You show me that I am clay
>    and make certain that I am dust.
I cry out, and you do not answer;
>    I am silent, and you do not care.
You look down at me with hatred
>    and lash me with all your might.
You toss me around in storm clouds,
>    straddle me on the wind.
And I know that you will destroy me
>    and lock me in the house of the dead.

Did I ever strike down a beggar
>    when he called to me in distress?
Didn't I weep for the wretched?
>    Didn't I grieve for the poor?
Yet instead of good came evil,
>    and instead of light there was darkness.

My innards boil and clamor;
>    the days of suffering have caught me.
I despair and can find no comfort;
>    I stand up and cry for help.
I am brother to the wild jackal,
>    friend to the desert owl.

My flesh blackens and peels;
     all my bones are on fire.
And my harp is tuned to mourning,
     my flute to the sound of tears.

I made a pact with my eyes,
     that I would not gaze at evil.
But what good has virtue done me?
     How has God rewarded me?
Isn't disgrace for sinners
     and misery for the wicked?
Can't he tell right from wrong
     or keep his accounts in order?

If I ever held hands with malice
     or my feet hurried to crime
(I will *prove* that I am innocent!
     I will make him see with his eyes!)—
if my legs strayed from the path
     or my heart followed my glance
     or a stain clung to my palms—
let strangers eat what I sowed
     and tear out my crop by the roots!

If my loins were seduced by a woman
     and I loitered at my neighbor's door—
let any man take my wife
     and grind in between her thighs!

If I scorned the rights of my servant
or closed my ears to his plea—
what would I do if God appeared?
If he questioned me, what could I answer?
Didn't the same God make us
and form us both in the womb?

If I ever neglected the poor
or made the innocent suffer;
if I ate my meals alone
and did not share with the hungry;
if I did not clothe the naked
or care for the ragged beggar;
if his body did not bless me
for the warmth of my sheep's wool;
if I ever abused the helpless,
knowing that I could not be punished—
let my arm fall from my shoulder
and my elbow be ripped from its socket!

If my land cried out against me;
if its furrows saw me and wept;
if I took its fruits without paying
or caused its tenants to sigh—
let thorns grow instead of wheat
and thistles instead of barley!

If I ever trusted in silver
or pledged allegiance to gold;

if I ever boasted of my riches
    or took any credit for my wealth;
if I saw the sun in its splendor
    or the bright moon moving
and my heart was ever seduced
    and I kissed my hand in worship;
if I laughed when my enemy fell
    or rejoiced when suffering found him
or allowed my tongue to sin
    by binding him in a curse;
if my servants ever spoke
    an unkind word to a guest
(for I never shut out a stranger
    or turned a traveler away);
if I ever covered my crimes
    or buried my sins in my heart,
afraid of what people thought,
    shivering behind my doors . . .

Oh if only God would hear me,
    state his case against me,
    let me read his indictment.
I would carry it on my shoulder
    or wear it on my head like a crown.
I would justify the least of my actions;
    I would stand before him like a prince.

# The Voice from
# the Whirlwind

THEN THE UNNAMABLE ANSWERED JOB
FROM WITHIN THE WHIRLWIND:

Who is this whose ignorant words
      smear my design with darkness?
Stand up now like a man;
      I will question you: please, instruct me.

Where were you when I planned the earth?
      Tell me, if you are so wise.
Do you know who took its dimensions,
      measuring its length with a cord?
What were its pillars built on?
      Who laid down its cornerstone,
while the morning stars burst out singing
      and the angels shouted for joy!

Were you there when I stopped the waters,
      as they issued gushing from the womb?
when I wrapped the ocean in clouds
      and swaddled the sea in shadows?
when I closed it in with barriers
      and set its boundaries, saying,
"Here you may come, but no farther;
      here shall your proud waves break."

Have you ever commanded morning
      or guided dawn to its place—

to hold the corners of the sky
    and shake off the last few stars?
All things are touched with color;
    the whole world is changed.

Have you walked through the depths of the ocean
    or dived to the floor of the sea?
Have you stood at the gates of doom
    or looked through the gates of death?
Have you seen to the edge of the universe?
    Speak up, if you have such knowledge.

Where is the road to light?
    Where does darkness live?
(Perhaps you will guide them home
    or show them the way to their house.)
You know, since you have been there
    and are older than all creation.

Have you seen where the snow is stored
    or visited the storehouse of hail,
which I keep for the day of terror,
    the final hours of the world?
Where is the west wind released
    and the east wind sent down to earth?

Who cuts a path for the thunderstorm
    and carves a road for the rain—
to water the desolate wasteland,
    the land where no man lives;

to make the wilderness blossom
 and cover the desert with grass?

Does the rain have a father?
 Who has begotten the dew?
Out of whose belly is the ice born?
 Whose womb labors with the sleet?
(The water's surface stiffens;
 the lake grows hard as rock.)

Can you tie the Twins together
 or loosen the Hunter's cords?
Can you light the Evening Star
 or lead out the Bear and her cubs?
Do you know all the patterns of heaven
 and how they affect the earth?

If you shout commands to the thunderclouds,
 will they rush off to do your bidding?
If you clap for the bolts of lightning,
 will they come and say "Here we are"?
Who gathers up the stormclouds,
 slits them and pours them out,
turning dust to mud
 and soaking the cracked clay?

Do you hunt game for the lioness
 and feed her ravenous cubs,
when they crouch in their den, impatient,
 or lie in ambush in the thicket?

Who finds her prey at nightfall,
    when her cubs are aching with hunger?

Do you tell the antelope to calve
    or ease her when she is in labor?
Do you count the months of her fullness
    and know when her time has come?
She kneels; she tightens her womb;
    she pants, she presses, gives birth.
Her little ones grow up;
    they leave and never return.

Who unties the wild ass
    and lets him wander at will?
He ranges the open prairie
    and roams across the saltlands.
He is far from the tumult of cities;
    he laughs at the driver's whip.
He scours the hills for food,
    in search of anything green.

Is the wild ox willing to serve you?
    Will he spend the night in your stable?
Can you tie a rope to his neck?
    Will he harrow the fields behind you?
Will you trust him because he is powerful
    and leave him to do your work?
Will you wait for him to come back,
    bringing your grain to the barn?

Do you deck the ostrich with wings,
    with elegant plumes and feathers?
She lays her eggs in the dirt
    and lets them hatch on the ground,
forgetting that a foot may crush them
    or sharp teeth crack them open.
She treats her children cruelly,
    as if they were not her own.
For God deprived her of wisdom
    and left her with little sense.
When she spreads her wings to run,
    she laughs at the horse and rider.

Do you give the horse his strength?
    Do you clothe his neck with terror?
Do you make him leap like a locust,
    snort like a blast of thunder?
He paws and champs at the bit;
    he exults as he charges into battle.
He laughs at the sight of danger;
    he does not wince from the sword
or the arrows nipping at his ears
    or the flash of spear and javelin.
With his hooves he swallows the ground;
    he quivers at the sound of the trumpet.
When the trumpet calls, he says "Ah!"
    From far off he smells the battle,
    the thunder of the captains and the shouting.

Do you show the hawk how to fly,
    stretching his wings on the wind?
Do you teach the vulture to soar
    and build his nest in the clouds?
He makes his home on the mountaintop,
    on the unapproachable crag.
He sits and scans for prey;
    from far off his eyes can spot it;
his little ones drink its blood.
    Where the unburied are, he is.


THEN THE UNNAMABLE ASKED JOB:

Has God's accuser resigned?
    Has my critic swallowed his tongue?


JOB SAID TO THE UNNAMABLE:

I am speechless: what can I answer?
    I put my hand on my mouth.
I have said too much already;
    now I will speak no more.


THEN THE UNNAMABLE AGAIN SPOKE TO JOB
FROM WITHIN THE WHIRLWIND:

Do you dare to deny my judgment?
    Am I wrong because you are right?

Is your arm like the arm of God?
    Can your voice bellow like mine?
Dress yourself like an emperor.
    Climb up onto your throne.
Unleash your savage justice.
    Cut down the rich and the mighty.
Make the proud man grovel.
    Pluck the wicked from their perch.
Push them into the grave.
    Throw them, screaming, to hell.
Then I will admit
    that your own strength can save you.

Look now: the Beast that I made:
    he eats grass like a bull.
Look: the power in his thighs,
    the pulsing sinews of his belly.
His penis stiffens like a pine;
    his testicles bulge with vigor.
His ribs are bars of bronze,
    his bones iron beams.
He is first of the works of God,
    created to be my plaything.
He lies under the lotus,
    hidden by reeds and shadows.
He is calm though the river rages,
    though the torrent beats against his mouth.
Who then will take him by the eyes
    or pierce his nose with a peg?

Will you catch the Serpent with a fishhook
    or tie his tongue with a thread?
Will you pass a string through his nose
    or crack his jaw with a pin?
Will he plead with you for mercy
    and timidly beg your pardon?
Will he come to terms of surrender
    and promise to be your slave?
Will you play with him like a sparrow
    and put him on a leash for your girls?
Will merchants bid for his carcass
    and parcel him out to shops?
Will you riddle his skin with spears,
    split his head with harpoons?
Go ahead: attack him:
    you will never try it again.

Look: hope is a lie:
    you would faint at the very sight of him.
Who would dare to arouse him?
    Who would stand in his way?
Who under all the heavens
    could fight against him and live?
Who could pierce his armor
    or shatter his coat of mail?
Who could pry open his jaws,
    with their horrible arched teeth?
He sneezes and lightnings flash;
    his eyes glow like dawn.

Smoke pours from his nostrils
    like steam from a boiling pot.
His breath sets coals ablaze;
    flames leap from his mouth.
Power beats in his neck,
    and terror dances before him.
His skin is hard as a rock,
    his heart huge as a boulder.
No sword can stick in his flesh;
    javelins shatter against him.
He cracks iron like straw,
    bronze like rotten wood.
No arrow can pierce his skin;
    slingstones hit him and crumble.
He chews clubs to splinters
    and laughs at the quivering spear.
His belly is thick with spikes;
    he drags the swamp like a rake.
When he rises the waves fall back
    and the breakers tremble before him.
He makes the ocean boil,
    lashes the sea to a froth.
His wake glistens behind him;
    the waters are white with foam.
No one on earth is his equal—
    a creature without fear.
He looks down on the highest.
    He is king over all the proud beasts.

**THEN JOB SAID TO THE UNNAMABLE:**

I know you can do all things
    and nothing you wish is impossible.
*Who is this whose ignorant words*
    *cover my design with darkness?*
I have spoken of the unspeakable
    and tried to grasp the infinite.
*Listen and I will speak;*
    *I will question you: please, instruct me.*
I had heard of you with my ears;
    but now my eyes have seen you.
Therefore I will be quiet,
    comforted that I am dust.

## EPILOGUE:
# The Legend

After he had spoken to Job, the Lord said to Eliphaz the Temanite, "I am very angry at you and your two friends, because you have not spoken the truth about me, as my servant Job has. So take seven bulls and seven rams and go to my servant Job and offer a sacrifice for yourselves. My servant Job will pray for you, and for his sake I will overlook your sin. For you have not spoken the truth about me, as my servant Job has." So Eliphaz the Temanite, Bildad the Shuhite, and Zophar the Namathite went and did what the Lord had commanded. And the Lord accepted Job's prayer.

Then the Lord returned all Job's possessions, and gave him twice as much as he had before. All his relatives and everyone who had known him came to his house to celebrate. They commiserated with him over all the suffering that the Lord had inflicted on him. As they left, each one gave him a coin or a gold ring.

So the Lord blessed the end of Job's life more than the beginning. Job now had fourteen thousand sheep, six thousand camels, a thousand yoke of oxen, and a thousand donkeys. He also had seven sons and three daughters: the eldest he named Dove, the second Cinnamon, and the third Eye-shadow. And in all the world there were no women as beautiful as Job's daughters. He gave them a share of his possessions along with their brothers.

After this, Job lived for a hundred and forty years. He lived to see his grandchildren and his great-grandchildren. And he died at a very great age.

# *Notes*

# A Note on the Text

*Job* probably dates from the seventh to fifth centuries before the common era. But the earliest Hebrew manuscript that survives was written some fifteen hundred years later. Through many centuries of oral and scribal transmission, corruptions are bound to occur even in the simplest text; and *Job*, because of its strange idiom and the extreme compression of its verse, must have seemed difficult even to the poet's contemporaries. Difficult, and scandalous. In several places, it is obvious that some scribe has deliberately altered a word, out of a pious desire to suppress Job's blasphemy. And there are numerous other errors that must be due to inadvertence or misunderstanding.

However these corruptions came into being, they are there, in plain view, and the translator can make only the most tenuous sense out of many verses, unless he emends them. Some emendations may require revision of every word in a line; but most are relatively simple, requiring the change of a letter or two. For example, in chapter 5, verses 6–7 in the traditional (Massoretic) text can be rendered:

> For pain does not spring from the dust
> > or sorrow sprout from the soil:
> man is born to sorrow
> > as surely as sparks fly upward.

Not only is the second verse a weak antithesis; it contradicts Eliphaz's entire argument that misfortune is *not* the common lot of man, as Job thinks, and is not part of the natural order, but is rather the direct result of an individual's wickedness or folly. Now the original written Hebrew consisted entirely of consonants; the vowel-points were added during the seventh century C.E. by rabbinic scholars called the Massoretes, following the then current tradition of pronunciation. A change in vowel-points here (*yulad* to *yolid*) yields a verse that fits well in the context:

> man gives birth to sorrow
> as surely as sparks fly upward.

Some emendations carry with them the authority of the Septuagint, the ancient Greek translation, which dates from the second century B.C.E. and follows a different, possibly older, textual tradition than the Massoretic text. The relation of the Septuagint to the Hebrew Bible is itself a highly complex matter; the translation is often paraphrastic, and there are many errors and lacunae. But sometimes the Greek will be crystal clear where the Hebrew is muddled or meaningless. A simple instance occurs in 23:13:

> For he [God] is in one, and who can turn him back?
> What he wishes to do, he does.

The first phrase has been interpreted, with varying degrees of strain, as meaning "he is of one mind" or "he is alone in power." But the Septuagint, instead of *b'ḥd*, "in one," reads as if it is translating *bḥr*, "has chosen":

> For he has decided, and who can turn him back?
> What he wishes to do, he does.

This makes perfect sense. And it is easy to account for the corruption: *r* was miswritten as *d*, which it closely resembles in Hebrew script; then some later scribe changed *bḥd*, which has no meaning, to *b'ḥd*.

Emendation is one way of reaching a true text. Another is comparative philology. (There is no way to recover *the* true text; all interpretations are to some extent arbitrary; and in the end the only method is one's own intuition.) Quite a few of the obscure expressions in *Job* can be elucidated by reference to cognates in other ancient Near Eastern languages. One example occurs in 39:21:

> He [the horse] paws in the valley and rejoices;
> in strength he goes out to meet the weapons.

The noun *'mq*, which usually means "valley" in Hebrew, means "strength, violence" in Akkadian and Ugaritic. There is an obvious parallel in the second line, and since parallelism is a structural principle of Hebrew poetry, the verse can with assurance be translated:

> He paws violently and rejoices;
> he runs furiously to meet the weapons.

Nevertheless, there are verses in *Job*, and even entire passages, which are so obscure, or where the text is so corrupt, that no solution seemed acceptable. I have omitted such verses when the omission did no damage to the continuity of the translation. I have also deleted scribal glosses and verses which seemed redundant or out of place, and have occasionally changed the order of verses as they appear in the Massoretic text.

The Elihu interlude, which has long been recognized as an addition by some later, much inferior poet, and the added Hymn to Wisdom that constitutes chapter 28, with its uncharacteristic stanza-form and its unruffled piety, have been left out as well.

Literal translations of *Job* may convey its sense more or less accurately, but no literal translation can hope to embody the grandeur and pulsing urgency of its style. In trying to make *Job* into a living poem, my primary obligations have been to the spirit of the original and to the rhythms of the English language. I have translated closely when possible, freely when necessary; and have not hesitated to improvise, on those few occasions when less drastic methods seemed inadequate.

# Selected Bibliography

BALL, C. J. *The Book of Job*, Oxford 1922.

BEER, G. *Der Text des Buches Hiob*, Marburg 1897.

BLOMMERDE, A. C. M. *Northwest Semitic Grammar and Job*, Rome 1969.

BUDDE, K. *Das Buch Hiob*, Göttingen 1896, 1913.

DELITZSCH, F. *Das Buch Hiob*, Leipzig 1902.

DHORME, E. *Le Livre de Job*, Paris 1926.

DRIVER, S. R., and G. B. GRAY. *A Critical and Exegetical Commentary on the Book of Job*, Edinburgh 1921.

EHRLICH, A. B. *Randglossen zur Hebräischen Bibel, Band 6*, Leipzig 1918.

GUILLAUME, A. *Studies in the Book of Job*, Leiden 1968.

HITZIG, F. *Das Buch Hiob übersetzt und ausgelegt*, Leipzig 1897.

PETERS, N. *Das Buch Hiob*, Münster-in-Westfalen 1928.

POPE, M. H. *Job*, New York 1965, 1973.

STEVENSON, W. B. *Critical Notes on the Hebrew Text of the Poem of Job*, Aberdeen 1951.

TORCZYNER, H. *Das Buch Hiob*, Wien 1920.

TUR-SINAI, N. H. *The Book of Job: A New Commentary*, Jerusalem 1957.

YELLIN, D. *Ḥiqrê Miqra'*, vol. 1, Jerusalem, 1927.

# Abbreviations

| | |
|---|---|
| A | Aquila |
| cj. | conjecture |
| LXX | Septuagint |
| MT | Massoretic text |
| Q | Qere' |
| Q tg | Qumran Targum |
| 𝔖 | Syriac (Peshitta) |
| 𝔗 | Targum |
| 𝔙 | Vulgate |
| Θ | Theodotion |
| Σ | Symmachus |
| > | lacking in |

| | |
|---|---|
| AJSL | *American Journal of Semitic Languages and Literature* |
| BCCT | *The Bible in Current Catholic Thought*, ed. J. L. McKenzie, New York 1962. |
| BH | *Biblia Hebraica*, ed. R. Kittel, 3d ed., Stuttgart 1937; 4th ed., 1974. |
| CBQ | *Catholic Biblical Quarterly* |
| GSAI | *Giornale della società asiatica italiana* |
| HUCA | *Hebrew Union College Annual* |
| JBL | *Journal of Biblical Literature* |
| JJS | *Journal of Jewish Studies* |
| JKF | *Jahrbuch für kleinasiatische Forschung* |
| JNES | *Journal of Near Eastern Studies* |
| JQR | *Jewish Quarterly Review* |
| JTS | *Journal of Theological Studies* |
| K-B | L. Koehler, W. Baumgartner, *Lexicon in Veteris Testamenti Libros*, 1st ed., Leiden 1958; 3d ed., 1967, 1974. |
| KJ | King James version |
| NEB | *New English Bible*, Oxford and Cambridge 1970. |

| | |
|---|---|
| PF | *Promise and Fulfilment: Essays Presented to S. H. Hooke,* ed. F. F. Bruce, Edinburgh 1963. |
| OLZ | *Orientalistische Literaturzeitung* |
| RSV | Revised Standard version |
| ThZ | *Theologische Zeitschrift* |
| VT | *Vetus Testamentum* |
| VTS | *Vetus Testamentum* Supplement |
| ZAW | *Zeitschrift für die alttestamentliche Wissenschaft* |

# Textual and Philological Notes

2:8    האפר   For the principal meaning, "dust," see K-B³ *ad loc.* The only biblical instance of the meaning "ashes" is Num. 19:9 f.

3:3    הרה   Read הֶרָה or הֲרִי (LXX). Literally, "the night which announced: 'It's a boy!'" MT is possible, but LXX seems superior for the following reasons:

     1. "Job's quarrel is not with his conception, but with his birth, with the fact that he has issued from the womb living into the world with its life of trouble and pain; to have been conceived, yet not to have been born, is indeed one of the two alternative fates—the silence of the womb or the silence of Sheol—that he desires: if his mother had miscarried, or if he had been stillborn, all would still, even in spite of his conception, have been well with him" (Gray).

     2. The night of vv. 7–9 seems to be the night of birth, since רננה almost certainly refers to the rejoicing at the birth of a child (cf. 38:7 f.; Jer. 20:15). Although גלמוד (v. 7) may mean the inability to conceive (thus talmudic גלמודה), it may just as well mean the inability to *bear* children (cf. Is. 49:21, שכולה וגלמודה); and v. 10, which has night as the subject of at least one of its hemistichs, is certainly a cursing of Job's birth rather than of his conception (cf. Is. 66:9).

     3. The emended verse observes a temporal sequence—from the day when Job was being born to the night when he was born (v. 10 appears to observe the same sequence).

6    הלילה   Read הַיּוֹם (cj. Hontheim); cf. v. 6b, before which 𝕊 inserts *ywmʾ hw.* This emendation restores the curse's remarkable symmetry: vv. 3a, 4–6, and 10a refer to the day, vv. 3b, 7–9, and 10b to the night; and

just as יהי חשך (cf. Gen. 1:3) introduces the cursing of the day, יהי גלמוד introduces the cursing of the night.

הלילה seems to have intruded from v. 7 and היום to have dropped out afterwards, perhaps because of יום in v. 5. The three stages in the development of the text would thus be: (1) היום (ההוא), (2) היום ההוא, הלילה (ההוא) הוא = LXX ἡ ἡμέρα (MSS εκεινη) καὶ ἡ νὺξ ἐκείνη, (3) הלילה ההוא = MT.

יחד    Point יַחַד (Σ, 𝔙, 𝕮, 𝕾, Saadia).

7    הנה    Delete (> LXX, 𝕾, 𝔙, 1 MS). This word may have been added, after the corruption in v. 6, by a scribe who felt uneasy about the repetition of הלילה ההוא.

8    יום    Schmidt's conjecture יָם (in Gunkel, *Schöpfung und Chaos*, Göttingen 1921, p. 59) is attractive, and G. R. Driver (VTS 3, 72) supports it by citing an Aramaic incantation: "I will cast spells upon you with the spell of the sea and the spell of the dragon Leviathan." But Fishbane (VT 21, 160 ff.) suggests that in the context of an incantation, wordplay and puns are to be expected. Thus we have אור ˜ ערר ˜ ארֹרי, יקו ˜ יקבהו; and יגאלהו ("claim; defile"), כמרירי ("blackness; bitterness"), יקבהו ("curse; pierce"), גיל ("tomb; exultation"), and perhaps יחד ("join; rejoice"). It is quite possible, then, that MT is correct, with a play on יָם: "a clever paratactic device for preserving two mythologems of the Dragon."

16    Transfer after v. 12.

לא    Point לֵא (Pope).

17    רשעים    Beer notes that this word and יגיעי כח are parallel expressions and that רגז in v. 26 has a passive meaning. "Therefore the רשעים here must be those disquieted by others. Already Ibn Ezra and Ramban explained רשעים correctly as המתנועעים, giving the root רשע here the meaning which many exegetes accept for ירשיע in 34:29. But רשע is not authenticated in Hebrew as a metaplasm of רעש. Therefore the reading רֹעֲשִׁים is to be preferred. Cf. Jer. 4:24."

22    גיל    𝕾, 1 MS read גַל. Guillaume (PF, 110) compares Arabic *gal*, "the interior side of a grave."

4:3    יסרת   Yellin cites Hos. 7:15, where חזקתי is parallel to (or a gloss for) יסרתי, and suggests that both verbs (and also אמץ) in their root meanings refer to tying or tightening, hence strengthening. For חזק, cf. Is. 22:21, 28:22, etc.; for אמץ, cf. 2 Sam. 15:12, Pr. 31:17, etc.; for יסר, cf. מוֹסֵר.

רבים   Point רְבִים (NEB). G. R. Driver compares Akkadian *rîbu*, "quaking," and Arabic *ra'ba(y)*, "to waver." Tur-Sinai compares Arabic *rwb*, "to take fright, be dumbfounded." Parallel to ידים רפות.

11    אבד   "This means 'to go forth alone,' said of the lioness parted from her cubs (cf. Deut. 26:5) and is in parallelism with יתפרדו, 'to go forth separately' " (Ehrlich; cf. 29:13, 31:19). For the image, cf. 38:41, where יתעו אבד means "to go astray" in אבד מבלי טרף = לבלי אכל. 1 Sam. 9:3,20; Jer. 50:6; Ez. 34:4,16; Ps. 2:12, 119:176. (But in Ps. 92:10 יאבדו is parallel to יתפרדו and probably means "to perish.")

13    תרדמה   Parallel to חזינות. "This passage, as well as Dan. 8:18 and 10:9, may fairly serve as proof that the specific meaning 'prophetic ecstasy, vision' which was attributed to the word תרדמה is still traceable as far back as the Hebrew linguistic consciousness of late-biblical times." See I. L. Seeligmann, *The Septuagint Version of Isaiah*, Leiden 1948, p. 53, for the biblical and midrashic evidence (also Fullerton, JBL 49, 347). Cf. especially Gen. 2:21 and 15:12, where תרדמה is translated by LXX as ἔκστασις and "evidently conceived as meaning a prophetic exaltation." It is interesting to see how Milton's subtle intuition led him into the scene in Eden:

> "Hee ended, or I heard no more, for now
> My earthly by his Heav'nly overpowerd,
> Which it had long stood under, streind to the highth
> In that celestial Colloquie sublime,
> As with an object that excels the sense,
> Dazl'd and spent, sunk down, and sought repair
> Of sleep, which instantly fell on me, call'd

By Nature as in aide, and clos'd mine eyes.
Mine eyes he clos'd, but op'n left the Cell
Of Fancie my internal sight, by which
Abstract as in a transe me<sup>+</sup>hought I saw,

Though sleeping, where I lay, and saw the shape
Still glorious before whom awake I stood . . ."

*Paradise Lost* VIII 452 ff.

By the same token, שעפים here means not merely
anxious thoughts, or even nightmares, but rather the
dread which may accompany visions or trances, as
LXX (φόβοι) correctly senses.

19    עש   Delitzsch compares Arabic ʿašš, Akkadian ʿašašu,
"bird's nest," and points עָש. Cf. 27:18, where the parallelism with סכה indicates that עש is the built rather
than the builder.

20    מבלי משים   Doubtful, even as an ellipsis, since the Hiphil of שים was not in use (Ehrlich). Dahood's reading
מִבְּלִי־שֵׁם שֶׁם is interesting and possible. I have followed
LXX's reading, παρὰ τὸ μὴ δύνασθαι αὐτοὺς ἑαυτοῖς
βοηθῆσαι, which probably = מבלי משיע (Merx; cf.
6:13, 26:2). But see Orlinsky, HUCA XXXV, 59 ff.

5:3    משריש   Read מְשָׁרֵשׁ (cj. Duhm).

ואקוב   I have followed LXX ἐβρώθη and ℨ wʾbdʾ,
which seem to read וַיִּקַּב (Cheyne) or וְרָקַב (Merx).
The person of the verb in MT may be due to a false
analogy with ראיתי.

5    קצירו   Read קָצְרוּ (LXX).

ושאף   LXX ἐκσιφωνισθείη, ℣ *bibent*. Read וְשָׁאֲפוּ
(Dhorme) or וְשָׁאֲבוּ (Graetz).

צמים   Read צְמֵאִים (A, Σ, ℨ, ℣, Saadia).

7    יולד   Point יֹלִד (Böttcher). See pp. 95 f. For *lamed* ac-
cusative in לעמל, cf. v. 2, 9:11, 12:23, 19:28. "It is evi-
dent that the first hemistich is going to give the affirmative parallel, since it repeats the word עמל and
contrasts אדם with אדמה. The presence of ל before עמל
has induced the pointing of MT and the versions,

which take יולד as a passive. Cf. the use of הוליד in Is. 59:4. The antithesis between the statement in v. 7, as emended, and that of v. 6 is thus clearly apparent'' (Dhorme).

15    מפיהם  Read פְּתָיִם (cj. Pope) or מֶפָּח (cj. BH⁴). Cf. ʊ, which adds *egenum*, and Saadia, who adds ʼ*lmˤpy*, as objects of the verb.

21    בשוט  Point בְּשׁוּט (Saadia): parallel to כי יבוא.

6:3    לעו Σ κατάπικροι, ʊ *dolore sunt plena*. See Sutcliffe, *Biblica* 31, 365 ff., who compares Arabic *laˤa*, ''to be anxious, fainthearted''; *lawˤah*, ''suffering, sorrow, despondency.''

6    חלמות ₂ℭ ברירא דחלמונא. See Dhorme, *ad loc.*

7    המה  Read זְהֵמָה (Wright; 3 MSS LXX βρῶμον). Cf. 33:20, which also has לחם as object. Still, כדוי לחמי is difficult, and Dhorme's conjecture זְהֵמָה כְּבֵדִי לחמי may be the best solution.

13    האם ℭ *hʼ*, ʊ *ecce.*

18–19  I have combined these verses.

21    עתה  Read אַתֶּם (LXX, ℭ).

   לא (Q לו)  Read עָלָי (ℭ); cf. LXX μοι ἀνελεήμονες (for this reading, see Orlinsky, HUCA xxxiii, 130 ff.). Most scholars accept Michaelis' emendation of כי to כן; but, as Stevenson remarks, it is more likely that vv. 15–20 refer to Job's kinsmen than to his three friends.

26    ולרוח  Point וּלְרַוֵּחַ and compare Arabic *rawwaḥa*, ''to give rest to'' (Guillaume). Questionable; but the grammar and parallelism seem to require a verb. McNeile's conjecture וּלְרִיב is another possibility.

7:4    Insert יום after מתי (LXX) and read וּמָתַי for ומדד (LXX). See Dhorme, *ad loc.*

6    תקוה  Ibn Ezra notes both meanings, ''thread'' and ''hope.''

15    מעצמותי  Read עַצְמוֹתָי (LXX, ℭ, ʊ). As מות is parallel to מחנק, so עצמותי is parallel to נפש. (LXX reads ממות, the first *mem* perhaps due to dittography or to parallelism with its reading מֵחֶנֶק.)

108

20      עלי   One of the eighteen acknowledged *tiqqunê sopherim*. LXX, perhaps correctly, reads עָלֶיךָ.

8:4      ביד   For the meaning "for, because of," see Gordis, JBL 62, 341 ff.

6      יעיר עליך   LXX δεήσεως ἐπακούσεταί σοι. For עיר = Semitic ǧjr, "watch over, guard," see Hartmann, VTS 16, 102 ff.; cf. Dan. 4:10. Yellin compares Deut. 32:11 and several verses in which שמר means "to be awake."

         נות   Yellin compares Arabic *nwy*, "intention"; cf. Jer. 31:23. G. R. Driver cites Hab. 2:5, יַנְוֶה (MT יִנְוֶה), "fulfilled his purpose."

8      וכונן   𝔖 *wtbyn*.

13      ארחות   LXX reads אַחֲרִית. Dhorme, in support of MT, cites Pr. 1:19.

14      אשר יקוט   Saadia *ḥabl eš-šams*. Read קֻשְׁרֵי קַיִט (cj. Peters). Of the various conjectures purported to mean "gossamer" or "web," this one is closest to MT. Unsubstantiated and questionable; but there is no better solution.

17      בית   K-B³ compares Aramaic, Syriac, Mandaic *byt*, "between." (1 MS בין.)

         יחזה   Read יֶחֱז = יֶאֱחֹז (cj. Budde).

21      עד   Point עֹד (Houbigant). LXX δέ.

9:16      קראתי ויענני   Point קָרָאתִי יַעֲנֵנִי (Ehrlich). (LXX = MT, as Orlinsky shows, HUCA xxix, 247.)

17      בשערה   Point בְּשַׂעֲרָה (𝔖, 𝔗).

19      יועידני   Read יוֹעִידֶנּוּ (LXX, 𝔖). "משפט here means not judgment, but argumentation. The Hiphil of עוד means 'to repeat an object,' hence 'to furnish a second example of it in oneself or in another' " (Ehrlich). Cf. Jer. 49:19, where יעידני is parallel to כמוני; Lam. 2:13, where אעידך (𝔙 *comparabo*) is parallel to אדמה לך.

20      פי   Read פִּיו (cj. Olshausen). See note to 13:15 below. This and אנכי in v. 35 are clearly *tiqqunê sopherim*.

27      אעזבה   G. R. Driver (VTS 3, 76) compares Arabic ʿaḍaba ɪv, "to make agreeable." Dahood (JBL 78, 304) compares Ugaritic ʿdb, "to arrange."

31 בשחת LXX ἐν ῥύπῳ, 𝔙 sordibus. Hoffmann's reading בְּשֵׁחֹת is probably correct. But see Pope, *ad loc.*

33 לא Point לָא (LXX, 𝔖; 13 MSS לוֹ).

34 ואמתו Point וְאֻמָּתוֹ (Dahood); cf. 13:21, 33:7.

35 אנכי Read הוא (cj. Torczyner, Ehrlich). Thus Seeligmann, VTS 16, 268.

10:1 עלי Read עָלָיו (LXX).

8 יחד סביב Read אַחַר סֹבֵב (LXX).

9 כחמר Read חֹמֶר (LXX: dittography).

16 ויגאה Read וְאֶגְאֶה (𝔖).

20 יְמֵי חֶלְדִי שִׁית (Q יְמֵי וַחֲדָל וְשִׁית) Read יְמֵי חֶלְדִי יָשִׁית (LXX, 𝔖). LXX ἔασόν με may indicate שְׁאֵה.

22 סדרים LXX φέγγος, which may = נְהָרָה (Schwally; cf. 3:4). But Schultens (*Liber Jobi*, Lugduni Batavorum 1737) compares Arabic *sdr*, "light."

11:2 הרב Point הֲרַב (LXX, Σ, 𝔗, 𝔙, Saadia).

4 לקחי LXX τοῖς ἔργοις, which may indicate לְכְתִּי.
היתי Read הָיִיתָ (cj. Ehrlich).

6 כפלים Read פְּלָיִם = פְּלָאִים (cj. Beer).

8 מה תפעל "This means 'what can you conceive?' Cf. Ps. 58:3 and Arabic *p'l* VIII" (Ehrlich).

10 יחלף Read יַחְתֹּף (cj. Graetz); cf. 9:12. LXX κατα-στρέψῃ seems to support this reading; but the relation of the whole hemistich in LXX to MT is unclear, and in 9:12 LXX translates differently.
ויקהיל "Condemn, literally 'call an assembly,' for the purpose of condemning a culprit" (Pope). Guillaume compares Arabic *qahala*, "to administer a severe rebuke."

11 ולא יתבונן 𝔖 does not translate לא; Θ, 𝔗, 𝔙 translate as an interrogative. Reuss's reading לוֹ may be correct.

12 פרא אדם "Gen. 16:12 shows that *pr' 'dm* is a unit. Dahood (CBQ 25, 123 f.) has shown that *'dm* is sometimes equivalent to *'dmh*, 'ground.' Accordingly, *pr' 'dm* would mean 'a wild ass of the steppe' " (Pope).

13 הכינות LXX καθαρὰν ἔθου.

17 תעפה Point תְּעֻפָּה (𝔖, 𝔗, 3 MSS).

18 וחפרת "Point וְחָפַרְתָּ and compare Arabic *ḥafara*, 'to shelter' " (Ehrlich).

12:2   עם  This word undoubtedly conceals a parallel to
חכמה. Reider (VT 4, 289 f.) compares Arabic ʿ*mym*
(pl. ʿ*m*), "complete, perfect, without deficiency." Dahood (*Psalms I*, New York 1966, pp. 112 f.; *Psalms II*,
New York 1968, pp. xxiii, 316) proposes a root ʿ*mm*,
"to be strong, wise," cognate with ʿ*mq*, and compares,
among other verses, 1 Sam. 17:42, Ez. 28:3, Ps. 89:20.
These explanations, though neither is entirely convincing, are less strained than Beer's emendation to
עֲרֵמִים or Klostermann's to הַיֹּדְעָם.

      תמות  Read תּוּמַת (A, Σ). Thus Mekhilta to Ex. 18:8. Cf.
36:4, 37:16.

8     שיח לארץ  Read שִׂיחֵי אֶרֶץ (cj. RSV).

17, 19   I have combined these verses.

18     מוסר  Point מוֹסֵר (𝔖, 𝔙).

21     מזיח  A *hapax legomenon*, not to be identified with מֵזַח.
Geers (AJSL 34, 132) derives it from Aramaic זוח, "to
be proud, overbearing"; cf. Ecclus. 8:11.

23     וינחם  Read וַיִּמְחֵם (cj. Ball). "Wright and Gray, who
accept the pointing וַיַּנְחֵם, postulate a meaning 'and
abandons them'; but the verb הניח, when it has as its
complement 'nations,' means 'leave in peace' (Jg.
2:23, 3:1). Again, one cannot argue on the basis of 2
Kg. 18:11, to give to וַיַּנְחֵם 'and leads them' the meaning 'deport,' for it is clear, in the light of 2 Kg. 17:6 and
the versions, that the word is to be pointed וַיַּנִּחֵם 'and
established them.' Ball's reading here is an excellent
parallel to ויאבדם" (Dhorme).

13:12     לגבי  Beer compares Syriac *gwb*, "to answer." Eitan
(AJSL 45, 203) cites the Arabic and Aramaic cognates.

14     על מה  Delete (> LXX: dittography).

15     דרכי  Read דְּרָכָיו (2 MSS). "This correction is necessary, because with MT the danger of the act in 15a is
too highly exaggerated. The case is altogether different, however, if Job is speaking here of criticizing
*God's* conduct" (Ehrlich). Moreover, הוכיח in *Job*
means either "to rebuke" or "to judge," and this
would be the only instance in the entire Bible of a

meaning "to justify." (According to Seeligmann's study of the root in VTS 16, 251 ff., such a meaning is improbable.) The aggressive connotation of אל פניו (cf. 1:11, 21:31; with דרכי one would expect simply לפניו) makes the emendation almost certain. "It is entirely possible that דרכיו was consciously altered to דרכי in order to weaken the expression. Similar modifications are not lacking elsewhere in the MT of Job. The *tiqqun sopherim* in 7:20, without doubt a conscious modification, brings a certain confirmation to this opinion. In our verse, the context is, precisely, more audacious than in 7:20" (Seeligmann).

21     ואמתך    Point וְאֲמָתְךָ (Dahood).

28     Transfer after 14:2.
         כרקב    Point כְּרֹקֶב (LXX, ⅁, ⅂).

14:3    ואתי    Read וְאֹתוֹ (LXX, ⅁, ⅊).

6      ויחדל    Read וַחֲדָל (Budde: 1 MS). Cf. 7:16, Jer. 40:4.

10     ויחלש    LXX ᾤχετο. Eitan compares Arabic *ḥalasa*, "to snatch away, carry off." See the fine discussion in his *A Contribution to Biblical Lexicography*, New York 1924, pp. 42 ff.

12c    Orlinsky (JQR 28, 57 ff.) demonstrates that this "is a gloss of לא יקיצו which could have come into existence only after the original meaning of יקיצו had been forgotten, and that יקיצו is an 'Arabism,' *qʾṣ*, 'to tear asunder.' These conclusions do away with all anomalies of meter, syntax, and style, and account for the rendering of LXX." I have translated 12b so that the statement appears more clearly as contrary-to-fact, rather than apocalyptic.

15:5    לשון    Point לְשׁוֹן (Blommerde). Parallel to פיך.

12     ירזמון    Read יְרוּמוּן (LXX, 1 MS).

18     כחדו מאבותם    Read כִּחֲדוּם אֲבוֹתָם (LXX).

22     וצפו (Q וצפוי)    LXX ἐντέταλται, which probably indicates וְצֻפּוּן.

23a    Read הוּא לְלֶחֶם אַיֵּה (or נֹעָד) נֹדָד (LXX). (But see Orlinsky, HUCA xxxv, 72 f.)

23b    בידו    Read פִּידוֹ (Wright; LXX πτῶμα).

24 Insert יוֹם חֹשֶׁךְ from v. 23 (LXX).

29 מִנְלָם There is no satisfactory explanation of this word. Dahood (BCCT, 60 ff.; after Zorell, after Saadia) compares Arabic *manāl*, "acquisition"; but his exegesis depends upon an understanding of אֶרֶץ as "underworld," a meaning which it does not have in any of its fifty-odd other occurrences in *Job*. I have followed LXX οὐ μὴ βάλῃ ἐπὶ τὴν γῆν ῥίζαν (*sic*: see Orlinsky, HUCA xxxiii, 136 ff.), which is probably a guess.

30 וִיסוּר LXX ἐκπέσοι, 𝔙 *auferetur*. Perles's conjecture וְיֻסְעָר may be correct.

   ברוח Point בָּרוּחַ (Beer).

   פיו Read פִּרְחוֹ (LXX).

32 תמורתו Transfer from v. 31 (LXX). LXX ἡ τομὴ αὐτοῦ. Point תְּמוֹרָתוֹ (Beer; cf. 𝔖) or read זְמוֹרָתוֹ (Driver).

   תמלא = תִּמָּל (LXX, 𝔖, 𝔙, Saadia).

16:4 אחבירה Finkelstein (JBL 75, 328 ff.) compares Akkadian *ḫbr*, "to make noise"; cf. Ps. 58:6, Pr. 21:9.

5 יחשך Read לֹא אֶחְשֹׂךְ (LXX, 𝔖).

7 There are two problems with MT: the stichometry and the person of the verbs. (God is nowhere else addressed in chapters 16–17, except possibly for the obscure 17:3 f.).

   הלאני השמות Point הֶלְאַנִי הָשַׁמֹּות (Tur-Sinai); cf. Ps. 46:9.

   כל עדתי (> LXX) Read (תְּקַמְטֵנִי) כָּל־רָעָתִי (cj. Duhm); עד in v. 8 may be responsible for the supposed corruption.

   Both these readings are questionable; but MT is certainly incorrect.

12 שלו Ehrlich's conjecture שָׁלֵם is attractive, though perhaps unnecessary.

18 מקום Here, "tomb," as in Ez. 39:11 (Dahood, BCCT, 61 f.).

21 ובן Read וּבֵין (5 MSS).

17:7,11 These verses have been salvaged from the wreckage of this chapter and transferred before 16:22, the most appropriate place left for them.

11     זמתי Read זַמָּת (cj. NEB).

מורשי LXX ἄρθρα. Beer compares Syriac *mrš'*, "cord." Wright emends to מֵתָרַי.

13     אקוה Dahood (*Psalms I*, 122) at Ps. 19:5 compares this verse, Ps. 40:2, and Ps. 52:11. "The root should be equated with *qawah* II, 'to collect.' The semantic bond between 'call' and 'collect' is well illustrated by *qōl*, 'voice,' which is cognate with *qāhal*, 'to gather,' . . . and by *qarā'*, 'to call,' but which denotes 'to gather' in the Arabic fifth form and in Ps cxlvii 9 and Prov xxvii 16."

15b    ותקותי Guillaume compares the Arabic cognate meaning "piety." LXX seems to read וְטוֹבָתִי.

16     בדי Read בְּיָדִי or עִמָּדִי (LXX μετ᾽ ἐμοῦ).

נחת Point נֶחָת (LXX, ⅗).

18:3   נטמינו Read נִטְמֹנוּ (3 MSS).

4      תעזב Dahood (JBL 78, 306) compares Ugaritic *'db*, "to arrange," and translates "rearranged." Cf. Ps. 46:3.

7      ותשליכהו Read וְתַכְשִׁילֵהוּ (LXX).

11     והפיצהו לרגליו "This phrase is usually rendered 'and frighten him at every step'—an inadmissible translation, for the Hiphil of פוץ never means 'frighten' (not even in Ez. 34:21, which is often cited in support of this meaning), but means at most 'scatter,' and as a rule takes a plural object. The real meaning of our phrase is 'and cause him to flow over his feet,' i.e. 'and make him piss in his pants out of fear.' For this meaning of הפיץ, cf. Zech. 1:17, Pr. 5:16, for the use of the Qal of this verb; and for the image, cf. Ez. 7:17: 'Every hand will tremble; / all knees will drip with urine'" (Ehrlich). G. R. Driver (ZAW 65, 259 f.) suggests that the verb is neither פוץ, "to be scattered" (= Arabic *faṣa(w)* IV), nor פיץ, "to depart" (= Arabic *faḍa*), but rather פיץ, "to make water" (= Arabic *faṣa(y)* IV).

12a    Thus Hitzig. Questionable, but supported by the parallel personification of איד. Cf. Ps. 38:18, where לצלע נכון means "stationed at my side" (parallel to נגדי תמיד) and אֲנִי is parallel to מכאובי (Dahood).

13  MT, with its bizarre imagery, is certainly corrupt. It is significant that even in the Ugaritic texts there is no mention of a "first-born of Death" (Sarna, JBL 82, 316).

In reconstructing the original text, one may begin with the fact that in the verse passages of *Job* (3:3–42:6) עור always appears with a parallel noun and that in three of its six occurrences it is parallel to בשר (7:5, 19:20, 26; cf. 10:11). So בכור is almost certainly to be emended to בְּשָׂרוֹ or בָּשָׂר, the corruption being due to the similarity between *shin* and *kaph* in the archaic script. Now בדיו is lacking in LXX and ℭ, and looks suspiciously like a variant of בדי in 13a. Since the corrected hemistich makes poor sense with it and good sense without it, it is to be deleted. For 13b, therefore, read יאכל בְּשָׂרוֹ מות. (LXX, reading יאכל בכור מות, correctly senses that מות is the subject and בכור the object, and so points בְּכּוּר.)

There are two indications that בדי is corrupt: the existence of a variant (and the textual tradition for בדיו itself is not clear, the Oriental Ketiv and 1 MS reading בדוי), and the difficulty of the phrase בד בדי עורו. בד means "idle talk" in 11:3 and may be corrupt in two other passages—probably in 17:6 and possibly in the difficult 41:4. But nowhere else in the Bible does it mean "limb," and such a meaning here is extremely doubtful. Since עורו is parallel to בשרו, a parallel to מות is likely. I have read דְּוַי. The verse as emended would thus read: יאֹכַל דְּוַי עוֹרוֹ / יֹאכַל בְּשָׂרוֹ מָוֶת. (For 13a, NEB reads יְאֻכַּל בִּדְוַי עוֹרוֹ.)

15  מבלי לו  Corrupt. I have adopted Dahood's emendation (*Biblica* 38, 312 ff.) to מַבֵּל* (cf. Akkadian *nablu*, Ethiopian *nabal*, Ugaritic *nblat*, "fire"). This is a questionable reading, and Θ's text may indicate that the *mem* is a late corruption. But it supplies good sense and parallelism, and other emendations are even less supportable.

19:13  הרחיק  Read הִרְחִיקוּ (LXX, A, Σ, ℭ).

15–16 I have combined these verses.

18     וידברו בי   Eitan (*A Contribution to Biblical Lexicography*, 33 ff.) compares Arabic 'dbr, "to recede, turn the back, flee." "In these verses, Job does not accuse anyone of active cruelty to him, such as mockery, calumny, denunciation, etc. But he does complain of his great aloneness. All abandon him, not out of spite or cruelty, but because of repulsion and loathing."

19     נהפכו בי   Penar (*Biblica* 48, 293 ff.) compares Ecclus. 6:11, the only other instance of this phrase, where יהפך בך is parallel to מפניך יסתר. Cf. 30:10a.

24     ועפרת   Read וְצִפֹּרֶן (cj. Budde); cf. Jer. 17:1. MT describes a process which scholars from Rashi on have failed to explain satisfactorily. For an impressive archeological and linguistic defense of the emendation, see Stamm, ThZ 4, 331 ff.

25–27 These famous verses are so filled with obscurities and corruptions that they are "impossible of textual solution on any theory" (Orlinsky, HUCA xxxii, 248). I have had to omit them and improvise drastically.

20:2     חושי   "The cognate roots חוש, חשש, which are common in mishnaic Hebrew, Aramaic, and Syriac, are used only of feeling pain, or of fear and apprehension" (R. Gordis, *Koheleth—The Man and His World*, New York 1968, p. 226.)

4     הזאת   Θ μὴ ταῦτα. Gordis (AJSL 49, 212 f.) cites the following verses, where questions seeking an affirmative answer occur without a negative: Gen. 16:13b, 1 Sam. 2:27, 17:25, 1 Kg. 22:3, Jer. 31:20, Amos 6:2.

6     שיאו   Guillaume (PF, 114) compares Arabic šawa, "the head or skull of a human being."

15 I have combined this verse with v. 18.

17     נהרי   Klostermann's emendation יִצְהָר is adopted by most modern scholars. But Chajes (GSAI 19, 181 f.) suggests that נהרי may be derived from the root נהר, "to shine," and means "oil" (thus יצהר צהר from צהר). The final *yod* is possibly a corruption due to נחלי in 17b.

18     כחיל תמורתו   The parallel hemistich suggests that MT

conceals a verb. Read כַּח לִתְמוּרָתוֹ (cj. Gordis). G. R. Driver compares Aramaic כחח, "to cough up phlegm."

יעלס Parallel to יבלע. Yellin compares mishnaic לעס, "to chew."

22 עמל Point עָמָל (LXX, $\mathfrak{V}$).

23 בלחומו The sense seems to require an object and to indicate that the *bet* is radical. I have followed LXX ὀδύνας, which may = חֲבָלִים (Merx; cf. ὠδῖνες 21:17) or בַּלָּהוֹת (Bickell; cf. 18:11, 27:20, 30:15).

26 טמון לצפוניו LXX αὐτῷ ὑπομεῖναι. Read לוֹ טָמוּן (Sieg-fried) or לוֹ צָפוּן (Dhorme).

27 Transfer after v. 28.

28 יגל Point יָגֹל (LXX, $\mathfrak{C}$).
יבול (1 MS יבל) LXX ἀπώλεια. Yellin compares Jer. 17:8, Is. 30:25, and Arabic *wbl*, "heavy rain," from which מבול also is to be derived.

29 אמרו Read מוֹרָא (cj. Beer).

21:8 Siegfried deletes לפניהם. Ball, followed by Dhorme, reads עֹמְדִים for עמם.

13 יבלו Read יְכַלּוּ (Q, LXX, $\mathfrak{S}$, $\mathfrak{C}$, $\mathfrak{V}$).
וברגע LXX ἐν ἀναπαύσει, $\mathfrak{C}$ ובמרגוע.
יחתו Point יֵחַתּוּ (Σ, $\mathfrak{S}$, $\mathfrak{C}$, $\mathfrak{V}$, Saadia).

20 כידו Guillaume compares Arabic *ka'da'ᵘ*, "calamity." But LXX τὴν ἑαυτοῦ σφαγήν, $\mathfrak{C}$ תביריה, $\mathfrak{V}$ *interfectionem suam* probably read פִּידוֹ or אֵידוֹ.

24 עטיניו Read עֲטָמָיו (cj. Bochart). LXX ἔγκατα, $\mathfrak{C}$ ביזוי, $\mathfrak{V}$ *viscera*.
חלב Point חֵלֶב (LXX, $\mathfrak{S}$, $\mathfrak{V}$).

30 יובלו This may not bear the meaning "to be saved," and perhaps Merx's conjecture יִצֵּל is correct.

22:11 או חשך Read אוֹר חָשַׁךְ (LXX).

12 וראה Point וּרְאֵה (Michaelis; cf. LXX, $\mathfrak{S}$).

15 עולם Point עַוָּלִם (Chajes).

17 למו Read לָנוּ (LXX, Q tg, $\mathfrak{S}$).

20 קימנו Θ ἡ ὑπόστασις αὐτῶν; cf. $\mathfrak{S}$, $\mathfrak{C}$, $\mathfrak{V}$. Read קִימָם (Yellin) or יְקָמָם (Michaelis).

23    תבנה   Read תֶּעָנֶה (LXX). The corruption seems to have been caused by anticipation of the apodosis, which does not come until v. 25.

24    ושית על עפר   Read וְשַׁת לֶעָפָר (cj. Dhorme); cf. Θ, 𝔖.
      ובצור   Read וּכְצוּר (Θ, 𝔖, 𝔗, 𝔙, Saadia, 65 MSS).

26    תתענג   G. R. Driver (VTS 3, 84) notes that תתענג is elsewhere translated by LXX as πεποιθέναι (Is. 58:14) and by 𝔖 as *tkal*, "trust" (27:10, Is. 58:14) and *sabar*, "hope" (Ps. 37:11). His comparison with Arabic *'anaja* may be justified; but in any case the meaning "trust" does seem appropriate in this context and may simply be an extension or modification of the normal sense of the verb. Cf. 27:10, where this meaning is even more appropriate.

30    אי נקי   Θ ἀθῷον, 𝔙 *innocens*. Delitzsch points אַי or אֵי. Sarna (JNES 15, 118 f.) compares Arabic *'ayyu*, "whoever" (cf. Dahood, *Biblica* 49, 363). According to Ibn Parḥon, the phrase is equivalent to אִישׁ נָקִי, which perhaps should be read.
      ונמלט   Read וְתִמָּלֵט (cj. Ginsburg).

23:2    מרי   Read מַר (𝔖, 𝔗, 𝔙).
      ידי   Read יָדוֹ (LXX, 𝔖).

7    משפטי   Point מִשְׁפָּט (LXX, 𝔖, 𝔙, 8 MSS).

10    אצא   Possibly related to the Ugaritic and Arabic cognates meaning "to clean; to shine." The most convincing examples of this meaning are Jg. 5:31, Is. 62:1, Ps. 37:6, 73:7 (Esh, VT 4, 305 ff.; Dahood, BCCT, 67). These verses, however, "are, like Ps. 19, related to a tradition of sun hymns in which the sun 'goes out,' as a hero, from his tent or chamber" (Fishbane). Alternatively, then, "shine" may be an extension of the normal meaning of יצא: "to rise (like the sun)" or "to go out (like the sun's rays)."

12    מחקי   Read בְּחֻקִּי (LXX, 𝔙); cf. Ps. 119:11. *Bet* and *mem* are easily confused in the archaic script. Or the corruption may be due to a false parallel between חק and מצוה.

13     באחד   Read בָּחַר (LXX). Already Ibn Ezra realized that this is the correct reading, but it was too dangerous to let out more than a hint: "Some say that the *bet* is paragogic; but the truth is that it is not, and is part of the root: for there is a great mystery here." Cf. Ps. 132:13, where בחר and אוה are in parallelism.

14     חקי   Read חֻקּוֹ (𝔖, 𝔙).

24:1     לא   Delete (>LXX).

2     LXX has ἀσεβεῖς as the subject. Merx's addition of רְשָׁעִים is probably correct.

5     הן   LXX ἀπέβησαν δὲ ὥσπερ, 𝔖 'yk, 𝔗 היך דין כ, 𝔙 *alii quasi*.

    בפעלם   Read לְפָעֳלָם (Σ, 𝔗, 𝔙, 7 MSS); cf. Ps. 104:23.

    ערבה   Point עֲרָבָה (Dahood); cf. Ps. 104:23.

    לו   Point לוּ (Guillaume).

6     I have combined this verse with vv. 10 and 11.

    בלילו   Read בְּלִיַּעַל (cj. Larcher). Questionable; but the standard emendation בַּלַּיְלָה is even less likely.

12     מתים   Point מֵתִים (𝔖, 1 MS).

13     ישבו   Point יָשְׁבוּ (LXX, 𝔖, 𝔙, 4 MSS).

14     לאור   Carey's emendation לֹא אוֹר (haplography) is probably correct. "MT could be retained only if אור had already developed its later (mishnaic) meaning of 'evening' " (Gray).

    יהי כגנב   Read יְהַלֵּךְ גַּנָּב (cj. Merx).

14c     Transfer before 15c.

25:2 f.     I have transferred these verses after v. 6 and inserted 26:5–14.

3     אורהו   Read אוֹרְבוֹ (LXX).

5     ולא   Read לֹא (𝔖, 𝔗, 59 MSS), as in 15:15.

    יאהיל   "God is the subject, ירח the object. The expression is one of the poem's not infrequent Arabisms and means 'he considers worthy'; cf. Arabic 'hl II and IV" (Ehrlich). There is a very close parallel in 15:15, where יאמין is almost equivalent to יאהיל here.

26:2–4     Insert before 27:2.

3     לרב   Point לָרֹב (NEB). Gordis (*Jewish Forum*, October 1945, 1) compares this word (perhaps originally רֻבֶּה,

MT being due to haplography) to Aramaic רובה,
"young man," which comes to mean "inexperienced,
foolish." Cf. נער in Pr. 1:4; also פתי, "fool" = Arabic
*fatta*, "young man."

12   רגע  "Comparison with UT, 67:1:1–2, *ktmḫṣ ltn btn brḥ*
*tkly btn ʿqltn,* 'When you smote Lotan the primordial
serpent, made an end of the twisting serpent,' shows
that *rgʿ* and *kly,* both of which are synonymous with
*mḫṣ,* are in turn synonyms. In numerous passages,
LXX understood *rgʿ* as 'destroy' " (Dahood, *Psalms I,*
182). Cf. Is. 51:15. Jer. 31:35.

13   שמים  Read יָם or מַיִם (cj. Ehrlich). "In the second half
of this verse, נחש בריח obviously designates a sea-
monster, and this suggests that the first half also was
originally about the sea." MT שמים may be a scribal
error, caused by confusion with, or inadvertent copy-
ing from, v. 11.

שפרה  This word seems to conceal a parallel to חללה
(cf. v. 12, where רגע is parallel to מחץ). Derivation
from the root שבר is not implausible, since *bet* and *pe*
are frequently interchanged (see Dahood, *Gregorianum* 43, 75). For the image of God's shattering the sea
or sea-monster, cf. 38:11, Ps. 74:13. (Tur-Sinai's reading ברוחו שם ים שפרה is doubtful, though it does have
the virtue of preserving MT, with its *lectio difficilior*.)

27:6   יחרף  Point יֵחָרֵף (NEB). Delitzsch compares Arabic
*ḥrp,* "to alter."

8–23   I have assigned this passage to Zophar, and reversed
the order of vv. 9–10.

8   ישל  Point יֵשַׁל = יִשְׁאַל (Schnurrer).

19   יאסף  Read יוֹסֵף (LXX, 𝔖).

28:1–28  "The chapter is an independent poem on the limita-
tions of human achievement and, in contrast, the in-
comparable and inscrutable wisdom of God, rather
than a speech either of Job, or, though this would
raise less difficulty, of one of his friends. It contains no
single obvious connection with the stage of the debate
now reached, and only in v. 28, which may refer

obliquely to 1:1, has it any connection whatever with any preceding part of the book. On the other hand, in the mouth of Job it anticipates, and that in such a way as to render nugatory, the speeches of God in chapters 38–40" (Gray, 232 f.).

29:4   בסוד   Read בְּסוֹדִי (LXX, Σ, 𝔖).

5b    Dhorme's addition of עָמְדוּ (עמדי transferred from v. 6b) is probably correct.

10    נחבאו   Guillaume (PF, 119) compares Arabic ḫabi'a, "(the fire) died out." But the word "may well be due to a scribe's eye looking by error at v. 8a" (Driver), and perhaps something like נִכְלָא (Duhm) or גֶּאֱלָם (Siegfried) ought to be read.

11–20    I have inserted this passage after v. 25.

17    אשליך   LXX ἐξέσπασα. G. R. Driver (AJSL 52, 163) compares Arabic šlk I, "to save oneself"; II, "to draw (sword from scabbard); to rescue (from misfortune)." BH³ emends to אֶשְׁלֹף.

18    עם קני   Read בְּזִקְנִי (Cheyne) or עִמִּי זָקֵן (Dhorme), following LXX ἡ ἡλικία μου γηράσει.

וכחול   It is unlikely that this word means "phoenix": "an allusion to the resurrection and future life of the phoenix, and the attribution to Job of the wish that he might in this respect be like the phoenix, is inconsistent with the point of view throughout attributed to him" (Driver). LXX ὥσπερ στέλεχος φοίνικος (cf. Ex. 15:27, Num. 33:9, Ps. 92[91]:13), 𝔙 sicut palma probably indicate the reading וּכְנַחַל (BH³). K-B¹ notes that in Num. 24:6 and Cant. 6:11 נחל may = Arabic naḫl, "palm tree"; and BH³ adduces the example of Ecclus. 50:12(14), where στελέχη φοινίκων translates כערבי נחל (reading possibly כַּעֲבֹתֵי, according to Driver). I have followed LXX and 𝔙 and read וּכְנַחַל for the following reasons: (1) כחול, "like the sand," seems too hyperbolic (contrast Gen. 22:17; also Ps. 139:18, where the statement is meant literally); (2) the imagery in the next verse is botanical; (3) the palm tree is a figure for the just man in Ps. 92, and here too one expects a living thing in the simile.

24   לא   Delete (Budde).

30:3   אמש   Probably corrupt. The likeliest of the emendations are אָמָם (Klostermann) and אֶרֶץ (Olshausen).

7   "The verse describes them 'misbegetting as they were themselves misbegotten'; the parallelism is then excellent; they bray, like donkeys under the excitement of lust (cf. the neighing of horses in Jer. 5:8), and copulate with no better bed or screen than the rough and scanty growth of the desert affords" (Gray).

11   יתרו (יתרי Q)   Read יֶתֶר or יִתְרָם (cj. Budde).

  פתח ויענני   Read פִּתְּחוּ וַיְעַנֻּנִי (cj. Budde: haplography).

12   רגלי שלחו   Delete. Possibly a variant of v. 11b.

13   יעילו   Read יַעֲלוּ (cj. Bickell).

  עזר   Ehrlich compares Arabic ʿzr, "to help" or "to hinder." Dillmann emends to עֹצֵר.

14   תחת   The meaning "like" is unsubstantiated elsewhere, except perhaps for 34:26 (thus 𝔙). But otherwise, unless one adopts G. R. Driver's proposal (AJSL 52, 163) of an equally unsubstantiated temporal usage, the sense is obscure.

15   תרדף   Point תֵּרָדֵף (LXX).

17   נקר   Point נֻקַּר (Budde) or read נֹקְרִים (cj. Dhorme).

18   יתחפש   Read יִתְפֹּשׂ (LXX ἐπελάβετό).

  כפי   Read בְּפִי (cj. Ehrlich).

  יאזרני   Thus Dhorme. Ehrlich emends to יְאַחֲזֵנִי.

19   הרני   Read תֹּרֵנִי (LXX ἥγησαι δέ με, 𝔗 אשׁוו יתי, 𝔙 comparatus sum). See Orlinsky, HUCA xxxv, 76 f. The root is ירה II, "to teach," not ירה I, "to throw"; parallel to אתמשל.

  חמר   Like עפר ואפר, this refers to the human body. Cf. 10:9.

20   עמדתי   "MT is correct, but it is to be understood as the opposite of אשׁוע and means 'to be silent'; cf. 32:16" (Ehrlich). Cf. also 37:14 and Josh. 10:13, where דמם means "to stop" (Gordis).

  ותתבנן   𝔙 correctly expresses the negative here. Perhaps לֹא in the first hemistich is a "double-duty" negative (Fishbane). Alternatively, read וְלֹא תתבונן (1 MS).

22 תשוה (Q תֶשִׁיָה) Point תְּשֻׁנָה = תְּשָׁאָה.

24 בעי Reider (VT 2, 129) compares Arabic *ʿayyun*, "unable, impotent (especially from disease)." But Wright's conjecture בְּעָנְי seems more probable. Cf. אביון, v. 25.

ישלח Read אֶשְׁלַח (LXX). ...שלח יד ב regularly implies hostility or violence; cf. 28:9, Gen. 37:22, 1 Sam. 24:11, etc.

להן שוע Read לִי יְשֻׁוֵּע (cj. Dhorme). "Since the נ of להן comes from בעני, we are left simply with לה. In the light of LXX (ποιήσει μοι τοῦτο), it seems indeed that the original text had לי. The ה of לה springs from combination of two *yods*, the one at the end of לי and the other at the beginning of יְשֻׁוֵּע (which later became שוע)" (Dhorme).

28 חמה Read נֶחָמָה (cj. Duhm).

בקהל A peculiar image, since in the rest of this passage Job is completely isolated. Beer may be correct in reading בְקוֹל; cf. Ps. 3:5, 142:2.

31:1 בתולה Read נְבָלָה (cj. Peake). A somewhat arbitrary emendation; but as Pope says, "the context calls for some more comprehensive term for evil." Cf. Ibn Ezra: כאילו כרתי ברית עם עיני שלא יסתכלו מה שאין לי צורך ואחר שלא אביט מה אתבונן על בתולה.

10 תטחן "According to our sages, this word refers to sexual intercourse" (Rashi).

יכרעון The Arabic cognate is used of a woman's sexual acquiescence (Pope).

31 לא Delete in both hemistichs (> LXX).

32 לארח Point לָאֹרֵחַ (LXX, A, ᵴ, ᵭ, ᵮ).

34 ואדם "דמם here means not 'to be silent' but 'to be still' or 'to sit, be motionless'; cf. Josh. 10:12 f., 1 Sam. 14:9" (Ehrlich).

35 לי שמע Read אֶל יִשְׁמַע (cj. Gray). (לי > Θ, ᵴ, 6 MSS.)

תוי ᵵ ריגוגי, ᵮ *desiderium meum*. Ibn Ezra: "Some say that this word lacks an *aleph*. The sense is, 'I desire that God answer me.' " G. R. Driver (AJSL 52, 166) compares Syriac *twt*' , "inclination," and suggests that there may have been a Hebrew תוה, parallel with אוה, "inclined," to which תָּוֶה may be referred.

38–40     Transfer before v. 24.

39     בעליה    Point בַּעֲלֶיהָ (K-B³). Equivalent to פעליה (Dahood, *Gregorianum* 43, 75).

32:1–
37:24     "These chapters were obviously written to occupy their present position in the book: as 32:1–6 explains, Elihu speaks when the three friends have ceased to reply to Job; and in the speeches Elihu rebukes Job and the friends alike; and from Job's previous speeches he cites actual words, or summarizes statements in them, in order to refute them. But it is scarcely less obvious that the rest of the book was not written with any knowledge of these speeches; and consequently that they formed no part of the original work. In contrast to Elihu's frequent direct reference to the friends and to Job, there is no reference, direct or indirect, in any other part of the book to Elihu; the Prologue gives the setting for the debate that follows, and explains how the three friends who subsequently take part in it come to be present, but it says nothing of Elihu, and the special prose introduction to Elihu's speeches only partially supplies the omission; it gives a reason why Elihu speaks, it gives no reason why he is present. Neither Job nor the friends take the slightest notice of Elihu's attacks on them, or of his arguments; his speech is of greater length than any that have gone before, but no one interrupts him while he is speaking, no one has a word to say of or to him when he has done. Job's last speech closes with an appeal to God to answer him, and God's reply opens with words obviously addressed to the person who has just finished speaking; since this cannot be Elihu but must be Job, God's opening admits of no intervening speech of Elihu. Finally, in the Epilogue God

expresses a judgement on what Job has said and what the three friends have said, but makes not the slightest reference to Elihu. Thus this entire section can be removed from the book without any sense of loss or imperfection in its construction being created" (Gray, xl–xli).

For stylistic differences between this section and the rest of the poem, see Gray, pp. xlii–xlviii. "The style of Elihu is prolix, labored, and somewhat tautologous: the power and brilliancy which are so conspicuous in the poem generally are sensibly missing. The reader, as he passes from Job and his three friends to Elihu, is conscious at once that he has before him the work of a writer not indeed devoid of literary skill, but certainly inferior in literary and poetical genius to the author of the rest of the book" (Driver, xlvii).

38:8    ויסך   Read וָאָסֶךְ (LXX).

10    ואשבר   Read וָאָשִׁית (LXX, 𝔖, 𝔙). Q tg ותשׁוה. Cf. 14:13.

11    ישׁית בגאון   Read יִשָּׁבֵר גָּאוֹן (LXX). 𝔙 and 𝔖 (*ttbr:* cj. Merx) = תשׁבר. It is clear that שׁבר and שׁית have been transposed in MT.

12–15   "The sense of this passage is clear except on two points: what are the 'wicked' doing here, where they seem to be quite out of place, and what can the 'high arm' be? For this, if it denotes the arrogant conduct of the wicked, is equally out of place in a description of approaching dawn. The reader will have noticed that the *ayin* in רשׁעִים, 'wicked men,' is 'suspended,' i.e. written above the line; this peculiarity suggests that the copyists may have suspected the word and have wished to indicate that it has an unusual meaning or has been intentionally altered" (G. R. Driver, JTS 4, 210).

Grimme (OLZ 6, 53 ff.) makes the interesting conjecture רְשָׁפִים "sparks, flames," here specifically the stars, and compares a Phoenician inscription in which *ršpm* appears to have the same meaning. As for זרוע

רמה, he identifies this with "the constellation Ox-shank, the ḫ-p-š of the Egyptians, i.e. Ursa Major."

G. R. Driver explains רשעים as the "evil" stars, or else as a corruption of שְׂעִירִים, the "hairy ones" (thus the Arabic cognate)—either alternative referring to the dangerous Canis Major and Minor. זרוע רמה would, also like its Arabic cognate, refer to the stars of the Navigator's Line, "extending like a bent arm across the sky from the horizon to the zenith."

14   ויתצבו   Read וְתִצָּבַע (cj. Beer).

20   תבין   Point תְּבִיֶן = תְּבִיאֵנוּ (Hoffmann).

24   אור   "This is the west wind, Akkadian *amurru*, in Babylonian pronunciation *awurru*, which latter form is rendered in Aramaic inscriptions by אור. Talmudic אוריה, 'west wind,' is the same word" (Tur-Sinai).

27   מצא   Read מְצִיָּה (cj. Beer); cf. 30:3.

30   יתחבאו   The root here is not חבא, "to hide," but rather חבא, "to congeal, harden," cognate with חמא (Hitzig). Thus 𝔖, 𝔗, 𝔙.

34   תכסך   Read תַּעֲנֶךָ (LXX). MT is probably the result of a scribal confusion with 23:11.

37   ישכיב   Foster (AJSL 49, 31) compares Arabic *skb*, "to pour out." Thus Orlinsky, JBL 63, 36 ff.

41   לערב   Point לָעֹרֵב (Wright). MT probably results from an inadvertent remembrance of Ps. 147:9. For the image, cf. Ps. 104:20 f.: there too the lions come out at night to hunt and roar piously. יתעו in 41c can hardly refer to young ravens; neither Ehrlich's explanation ( = "stagger") nor G. R. Driver's in AJSL 52, 168 (תעע, "to guffaw, croak") is convincing, and Beer's emendation יִפְעוּ is doubtful at best. Furthermore, 4:11 provides a strikingly similar image of young lions roaming because of hunger. ציד is used of lions in vv. 39a and 10:16. Finally, it is unlikely that lions and ravens would be juxtaposed here, especially since the six descriptions in chapter 39 are all integral and at least four verses long.

39:10   Read הֲתִקְשֹׁר בַּעֲנָקוֹ עֵבֹת/אִם יְשַׂדֵּד תְּלָמִים אַחֲרֶיךָ (LXX). Cf.

התקטר (  ב) ניריה Q tg (M. Sokoloff, *The Targum to Job From Qumran Cave XI*, Ramat-Gan 1974, p. 90). See the fine discussion by Dhorme, *ad loc.*

12    זרעך וגרנך   Read וְזַרְעֲךָ גָּרְנְךָ (cj. Bickell); cf. LXX.

13    If חסידה is the name of a bird, either it is ironic or vv. 14–18 refer just to the רננים; śó for clarity's sake I have combined birds. The apparently interrogative form of 13b lends some support to Ibn Ezra's paraphrase of 13a (והתעם האתה נתת לרננים כנף), which I have followed (thus KJ; cf. Saadia). MT is unintelligible, the versions guess, Θ gives up and transliterates the difficult words, and there are no satisfactory emendations. I would prefer to omit this verse; but because of its position, some attempt at meaning is necessary.

14    תעזב   Dahood (JBL 78, 307 f.) compares Ugaritic ʿdb, "to arrange, place."

19    רעמה   Read אימה (LXX). I have transposed these two nouns in vv. 19–20, following a conjecture of Ball's. The root רעם always means a loud noise (contrast 1 Sam. 1:6, Ez. 27:35, where the root is different) and is appropriate in describing the "glorious snorting," v. 20. The association of הוד with thunder in 40:19 f. and Is. 30:30 is additional support for this reading. (See Dhorme, *ad loc.*, for a defense of the now standard translation "mane"; though this is weakened by the presence of רעם in v. 25.)

20    אימה   Read רעמה.

21    בעמק   Gordon (JKF 2, 56) compares Akkadian ʿmq, "to be strong," Ugaritic bʿmq "violently."

24    כי קול   1 MS reads בְּקוֹל.
      יאמין   Guillaume compares Arabic ʾamina, "to be quiet."

40:2   הרב   Point הָרָב (Σ, ℭ, ʊ).
       יסור   Point יָסוּר (Θ, ʊ).

15    בהמות   For the mythological nature of the two great beasts, see Pope, *ad loc.*

17    זנבו   A euphemism, as Albertus Magnus recognized:

" 'Tail' here stands for the genital member" (see J. Steinmann, *Le Livre de Job*, Paris 1955, pp. 334 ff.). זנב has this meaning also in *Tanhuma Ki Tetse* 10 (Jastrow, *Dictionary of the Talmud, ad loc.*). The same transference occurs in many other languages (e.g., Greek, German, and Chinese).

פחדו ‎ ℌ *testiculorum eius*, ℭ פחדוה. Natan ben Yehiel, in his *Arukh*, quotes some manuscript Targumim which read גוברריה ושעבבוזהי, "his penis and testicles" (cited by Delitzsch).

19    העשו יגש חרבו   MT is meaningless. Read הֶעָשׂוּי לְשַׂחֶק בּוֹ (= LXX πεποιημένον ἐγκαταπαίζεσθαι ὑπὸ τῶν ἀγγέλων αὐτοῦ). Cf. Ps. 104:26b, לויתן זה יצרת לשחק בו, where LXX translates ὃν ἔπλασας ἐμπαίζειν αὐτῷ. It is obvious that the two translators were working independently, and it is unlikely that the translator of *Job*, reading MT and unable to deal with it, should have substituted a verse difficult or troubling enough to require paraphrase. As for MT, the corruption from the original text is, as Torczyner observes, easily accounted for: העשוי(ג)שח(ר)בו. (*Lamed* and *gimel*, *qoph* and *resh*, are more commonly confused in the archaic script.)

23    יעשק   LXX ἐὰν γένηται πλήμμυρα. According to BH³, this = יִשְׁפַּע (πλήμμυρα = שֶׁפַע in Aquila's Deut. 33:19, Is. 60:6). But emendation may not be necessary. "This עשק is to be distinguished from the identical word meaning 'to oppress.' The latter corresponds to Arabic *'sq*, while this word is etymologically related to *ġsq* and means 'to overflow' " (Ehrlich). Dhorme compares Akkadian *ešqu*, "strong." LXX is certainly correct, whatever relation it has to MT.

ירדן   "Flowing water, as in Mandaean, with no reference to the Jordan" (Guillaume, PF, 126). " 'Jordan' is not a proper noun but seems to be an East Mediterranean word for river. Cf. Iardanos in *Odyssey* 3:291 f., *Iliad* 7:135" (C. H. Gordon, *Before the Bible*, New York

1962, pp. 284 f.). Ps. 114:3 is conclusive evidence: יַרְדֵּן is parallel to יָם, and both hemistichs refer to the parting of the Red Sea.

24 Insert מִי הוּא (cj. Budde: haplography). Questionable; but MT has to be corrected somehow.

בְּקָמֹשִׁים במוקשים Q tg בחכה. Ehrlich's conjecture may be correct.

41:2 לפני Read לְפָנָיו (33 MSS, 𝕿ᴹˢˢ).

3 הקדימני Read הִקְדִּימוֹ (cj. Gunkel).
ואשלם Read וַיְשַׁלֵּם (LXX).
לי Read מִי (cj. Westermann). Gunkel's conjecture לֹא is another possibility.

5 רסנו Read סִרְיֹנוֹ (LXX).

12 ואגמן Read וְאֹגֶם (Bickell: dittography).

15–16 I have combined these verses.

17 Insert after v. 20.
אלים Read גַּלִּים (cj. Mandelkern).
משברים Read מִשְׁבְּרֵי יָם (cj. Buhl); cf. Ps. 93:4.
יתחטאו K-B³ compares Ethiopic ḥṭ', "to withdraw." Pope compares Arabic ḥṭ', "to cast down."

18 מסע ושריה Both words are *hapax legomena;* the former is listed in K-B¹ as "unexplained." Read מַסִּיעָה שִׁרְיָה (cj. Peters). "The series of three nouns beside חרב in 18a is suspicious, מסע meaning 'missile' doubtful, שריה meaning 'arrow' or 'javelin' also doubtful, and שדיה = 'spear' verified only from the Syriac. However, in the light of שריון and שרין, there is little doubt about שריה = 'armor.' The phrase מַסִּיעָה שִׁרְיָה (or מַסִּיעַ שִׁרְיוֹן) would be quite suitable. For נסע Hiphil = 'to repel,' cf. 2 Kg. 4:4 and the usual meaning of the verb, 'to cause to depart' " (Peters).

20 יבריחנו LXX τρώσῃ. Here הבריח means "to wound" (Ehrlich at 20:24). G. R. Driver (VTS 3, 81) compares Arabic *baraḥa,* "to bruise." Cf. 20:24 (pointing יִבְרַח, with Ehrlich), 27:22, Pr. 19:26.

42:6 See Introduction, p. xxxii.
אמאס See Kuyper, VT 9, 91 ff. Thus K-B³.

ונחמתי נחם occurs nine more times in *Job*, always with the sense "to comfort."

עפר ואפר This phrase is found only here, in 30:19, Gen. 18:27, and Ecclus. 10:9, and always refers to the human body, which is "wholly dust" (K-B³). It was correctly understood by LXX (ἥγημαι δὲ ἐμαυτὸν γῆν καὶ σποδόν) and Q tg (ואהוא לעפר וקטם).

There is a striking parallel in Ps. 103:13–14, where God is said to have compassion on men precisely because he knows they are made of dust.

# Verses Deleted or Omitted

*Deletions* (glosses, interpolations, verses out of place):
1:22; 2:10d; 5:10; 6:10c,14; 9:21; 10:3c,15c,22b; 12:3b,4–6,22;
13:16; 14:4,12c,14a; 15:30a,31; 16:8,9c–11; 17:8–10,12; 19:28–
29; 20:23a; 21:16,22; 22:8,18; 23:8–9; 24:9; 28:1 28; 31:11 12,
23,28,40c; 32:1–37:24; 38:36; 40:7.

*Omissions:*
3:18; 4:21; 5:5b,12,22; 6:4b,27,29; 7:11b; 9:32; 10:1c,17; 13:19;
14:5c,17,19b; 15:19,28c; 16:20; 17:1–6; 18:4a,6,9,14,19; 19:12,
20,25–27; 20:10,24,25,26c; 21:17c,33c; 22:29; 24:13,16a,18–25;
26:9; 27:4,7,11–12,15,22; 29:20,25c; 31:18,34b; 38:15; 40:20,22;
41:4,7–9,11.

# Acknowledgments

Michael Fishbane went over an early version of the notes. Chana Bloch read the translation several times with subtlety and meticulousness. Joel Conarroe, Frederick Feirstein, and T. Carmi also made useful suggestions. My friend, neighbor, and running coach, Thomas Farber, helped improve the Introduction. I am grateful to them all.

And to Vicki.

Design by David Bullen
Typeset in Mergenthaler Palatino
by Auto-Graphics
Printed by Maple-Vail